Presented by

Peel Memorial Trustees

June , 1899.

WORKING MEN'S COLLEGE.

LIBRARY REGULATIONS.

The Library is open every weekday evening, from 7 to 10.30 o'clock, except on Saturdays, when it closes at 9.

RULE I.
Books can be borrowed from the Library any evening, and must be returned within three weeks. Certain books of reference cannot be borrowed.

RULE II.
Only one book can be borrowed at a time. Any Member keeping a book beyond three weeks will be liable to a fine of one penny per diem.

RULE III.
Any Member losing or damaging a book will be required to make good such loss or damage.

RULE IV.
Books must not be replaced on the shelves by readers, but must be left on the tables.

X 07966

ENGLISH SEAMEN

IN THE SIXTEENTH CENTURY

ENGLISH SEAMEN

IN

THE SIXTEENTH CENTURY

LECTURES DELIVERED AT OXFORD
EASTER TERMS 1893-4

BY

JAMES ANTHONY FROUDE

𝔑𝔢𝔴 𝔍𝔪𝔭𝔯𝔢𝔰𝔰𝔦𝔬𝔫

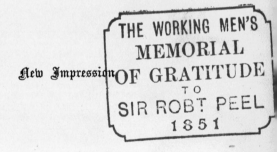
LONGMANS, GREEN, AND CO.
LONDON AND BOMBAY
1898

BIBLIOGRAPHICAL NOTE

First Edition, 8vo, March 1895.
Reprinted, Crown 8vo, May 1895, January
1896, December 1896, August 1898.

CONTENTS

—◇—

ENGLISH SEAMEN

IN

THE SIXTEENTH CENTURY

LECTURE I

THE SEA CRADLE OF THE REFORMATION

JEAN PAUL, the German poet, said that God
had given to France the empire of the land,
to England the empire of the sea, and to his own
country the empire of the air. The world has
changed since Jean Paul's days. The wings of
France have been clipped; the German Empire
has become a solid thing; but England still
holds her watery dominion; Britannia does still
rule the waves, and in this proud position she
has spread the English race over the globe; she

B

has created the great American nation; she is peopling new Englands at the Antipodes; she has made her Queen Empress of India; and is in fact the very considerable phenomenon in the social and political world which all acknowledge her to be. And all this she has achieved in the course of three centuries, entirely in consequence of her predominance as an ocean power. Take away her merchant fleets; take away the navy that guards them: her empire will come to an end; her colonies will fall off, like leaves from a withered tree; and Britain will become once more an insignificant island in the North Sea, for the future students in Australian and New Zealand universities to discuss the fate of in their debating societies.

How the English navy came to hold so extraordinary a position is worth reflecting on. Much has been written about it, but little, as it seems to me, which touches the heart of the matter. We are shown the power of our country growing and expanding. But how it grew, why, after a sleep of so many hundred years, the genius of our Scandinavian forefathers suddenly sprang

again into life—of this we are left without
explanation.

The beginning was undoubtedly the defeat of
the Spanish Armada in 1588. Down to that time
the sea sovereignty belonged to the Spaniards,
and had been fairly won by them. The conquest
of Granada had stimulated and elevated the
Spanish character. The subjects of Ferdinand
and Isabella, of Charles V. and Philip II., were
extraordinary men, and accomplished extraordinary
things. They stretched the limits of the known
world; they conquered Mexico and Peru; they
planted their colonies over the South American
continent; they took possession of the great West
Indian islands, and with so firm a grasp that
Cuba at least will never lose the mark of the
hand which seized it. They built their cities as
if for eternity. They spread to the Indian Ocean,
and gave their monarch's name to the *Philippines.*
All this they accomplished in half a century, and,
as it were, they did it with a single hand; with
the other they were fighting Moors and Turks
and protecting the coast of the Mediterranean
from the corsairs of Tunis and Constantinople.

They had risen on the crest of the wave, and
with their proud *Non sufficit orbis* were looking
for new worlds to conquer, at a time when the
bark of the English water-dogs had scarcely been
heard beyond their own fishing-grounds, and the
largest merchant vessel sailing from the port of
London was scarce bigger than a modern coasting
collier. And yet within the space of a single
ordinary life these insignificant islanders had
struck the sceptre from the Spaniards' grasp and
placed the ocean crown on the brow of their own
sovereign. How did it come about? What
Cadmus had sown dragons' teeth in the furrows
of the sea for the race to spring from who manned
the ships of Queen Elizabeth, who carried the
flag of their own country round the globe, and
challenged and fought the Spaniards on their
own coasts and in their own harbours?

The English sea power was the legitimate
child of the Reformation. It grew, as I shall
show you, directly out of the new despised Protestantism. Matthew Parker and Bishop Jewel,
the judicious Hooker himself, excellent men as
they were, would have written and preached to

small purpose without Sir Francis Drake's cannon
to play an accompaniment to their teaching.
And again, Drake's cannon would not have roared
so loudly and so widely without seamen already
trained in heart and hand to work his ships and
level his artillery. It was to the superior seamanship, the superior quality of English ships
and crews, that the Spaniards attributed their
defeat. Where did these ships come from?
Where and how did these mariners learn their
trade? Historians talk enthusiastically of the
national spirit of a people rising with a united
heart to repel the invader, and so on. But national
spirit could not extemporise a fleet or produce
trained officers and sailors to match the conquerors of Lepanto. One slight observation I
must make here at starting, and certainly with
no invidious purpose. It has been said confidently,
it has been repeated, I believe, by all modern
writers, that the Spanish invasion suspended in
England the quarrels of creed, and united Protestants and Roman Catholics in defence of their
Queen and country. They remind us especially
that Lord Howard of Effingham, who was Eliza-

beth's admiral, was himself a Roman Catholic.
But was it so? The Earl of Arundel, the head
of the House of Howard, was a Roman Catholic,
and he was in the Tower praying for the success
of Medina Sidonia. Lord Howard of Effingham
was no more a Roman Catholic than—I hope I
am not taking away their character—than the
present Archbishop of Canterbury or the Bishop
of London. He was a Catholic, but an English
Catholic, as those reverend prelates are. Roman
Catholic he could not possibly have been, nor anyone who on that great occasion was found on the
side of Elizabeth. A Roman Catholic is one who
acknowledges the Roman Bishop's authority. The
Pope had excommunicated Elizabeth, had pronounced her deposed, had absolved her subjects
from their allegiance, and forbidden them to fight
for her. No Englishman who fought on that
great occasion for English liberty was, or could
have been, in communion with Rome. Loose
statements of this kind, lightly made, fall in
with the modern humour. They are caught up,
applauded, repeated, and pass unquestioned into
history. It is time to correct them a little.

1 have in my possession a detailed account of
the temper of parties in England, drawn up in
the year 1585, three years before the Armada
came. The writer was a distinguished Jesuit.
The account itself was prepared for the use of
the Pope and Philip, with a special view to the
reception which an invading force would meet
with, and it goes into great detail. The people
of the towns—London, Bristol, &c.—were, he says,
generally heretics. The peers, the gentry, their
tenants, and peasantry, who formed the immense
majority of the population, were almost universally Catholics. But this writer distinguishes
properly among Catholics. There were the
ardent impassioned Catholics, ready to be confessors and martyrs, ready to rebel at the first
opportunity, who had renounced their allegiance,
who desired to overthrow Elizabeth and put the
Queen of Scots in her place. The number of
these, he says, was daily increasing, owing to the
exertions of the seminary priests; and plots, he
boasts, were being continually formed by them to
murder the Queen. There were Catholics of
another sort, who were papal at heart, but went

with the times to save their property; who looked
forward to a change in the natural order of things,
but would not stir of themselves till an invading
army actually appeared. But all alike, he insists,
were eager for a revolution. Let the Prince of
Parma come, and they would all join him; and
together these two classes of Catholics made
three-fourths of the nation.

'The only party,' he says (and this is really
noticeable), 'the only party that would fight to
death for the Queen, the only real friends she
had, were the *Puritans* (it is the first mention of
the name which I have found), the Puritans of
London, the Puritans of the sea towns.' These
he admits were dangerous, desperate, determined
men. The numbers of them, however, were
providentially small.

The date of this document is, as I said, 1585,
and I believe it generally accurate. The only
mistake is that among the Anglican Catholics
there were a few to whom their country was as
dear as their creed—a few who were beginning to
see that under the Act of Uniformity Catholic
doctrine might be taught and Catholic ritual

practised; who adhered to the old forms of religion, but did not believe that obedience to the Pope was a necessary part of them. One of these was Lord Howard of Effingham, whom the Queen placed in his high command to secure the wavering fidelity of the peers and country gentlemen. But the force, the fire, the enthusiasm came (as the Jesuit saw) from the Puritans, from men of the same convictions as the Calvinists of Holland and Rochelle; men who, driven from the land, took to the ocean as their natural home, and nursed the Reformation in an ocean cradle. How the seagoing population of the North of Europe took so strong a Protestant impression it is the purpose of these lectures to explain.

Henry VIII. on coming to the throne found England without a fleet, and without a conscious sense of the need of one. A few merchant hulks traded with Bordeaux and Cadiz and Lisbon; hoys and fly-boats drifted slowly backwards and forwards between Antwerp and the Thames. A fishing fleet tolerably appointed went annually to Iceland for cod. Local fishermen worked the

North Sea and the Channel from Hull to Falmouth. The Chester people went to Kinsale for herrings and mackerel: but that was all—the nation had aspired to no more.

Columbus had offered the New World to Henry VII. while the discovery was still in the air. He had sent his brother to England with maps and globes, and quotations from Plato to prove its existence. Henry, like a practical Englishman, treated it as a wild dream.

The dream had come from the gate of horn. America was found, and the Spaniard, and not the English, came into first possession of it. Still, America was a large place, and John Cabot the Venetian with his son Sebastian tried Henry again. England might still be able to secure a slice. This time Henry VII. listened. Two small ships were fitted out at Bristol, crossed the Atlantic, discovered Newfoundland, coasted down to Florida looking for a passage to Cathay, but could not find one. The elder Cabot died; the younger came home. The expedition failed, and no interest had been roused.

With the accession of Henry VIII. a new era

had opened—a new era in many senses. Printing was coming into use—Erasmus and his companions were shaking Europe with the new learning, Copernican astronomy was changing the level disk of the earth into a revolving globe, and turning dizzy the thoughts of mankind. Imagination was on the stretch. The reality of things was assuming proportions vaster than fancy had dreamt, and unfastening established belief on a thousand sides. The young Henry was welcomed by Erasmus as likely to be the glory of the age that was opening. He was young, brilliant, cultivated, and ambitious. To what might he not aspire under the new conditions! Henry VIII. was all that, but he was cautious and looked about him. Europe was full of wars in which he was likely to be entangled. His father had left the treasury well furnished. The young King, like a wise man, turned his first attention to the broad ditch, as he called the British Channel, which formed the natural defence of the realm. The opening of the Atlantic had revolutionised war and seamanship. Long voyages required larger vessels. Henry was the first prince to see the place which gunpowder was going to hold in wars. In his first years he repaired his dockyards, built new ships on improved models, and imported Italians to cast him new types of cannon. 'King Harry loved a man,' it was said, and knew a man when he saw one. He made acquaintance with sea captains at Portsmouth and Southampton. In some way or other he came to know one Mr. William Hawkins, of Plymouth, and held him in especial esteem. This Mr. Hawkins, under Henry's patronage, ventured down to the coast of Guinea and brought home gold and ivory; crossed over to Brazil; made friends with the Brazilian natives; even brought back with him the king of those countries, who was curious to see what England was like, and presented him to Henry at Whitehall.

Another Plymouth man, Robert Thorne, again with Henry's help, went out to look for the North-west passage which Cabot had failed to find. Thorne's ship was called the *Dominus Vobiscum*, a pious aspiration which, however, secured no success. A London man, a Master Hore, tried next. Master Hore, it is said, was given to cosmography,

was a plausible talker at scientific meetings, and
so on.   He persuaded 'divers young lawyers'
(briefless barristers, I suppose) and other gentlemen—altogether a hundred and twenty of them
—to join him.   They procured two vessels at
Gravesend.   They took the sacrament together
before sailing.   They apparently relied on Providence to take care of them, for they made little
other preparation.   They reached Newfoundland,
but their stores ran out, and their ships went on
shore.   In the land of fish they did not know how
to use line and bait.   They fed on roots and
bilberries, and picked fish-bones out of the ospreys'
nests.   At last they began to eat one another—
careless of Master Hore, who told them they would
go to unquenchable fire.   A French vessel came
in.   They seized her with the food she had on
board and sailed home in her, leaving the French
crew to their fate.   The poor French happily
found means of following them.   They complained
of their treatment, and Henry ordered an inquiry ;
but finding, the report says, the great distress
Master Hore's party had been in, was so moved
with pity, that he did not punish them, but

out of his own purse made royal recompense to
the French.

Something better than gentlemen volunteers
was needed if naval enterprise was to come to
anything in England.   The long wars between
Francis I. and Charles V. brought the problem
closer.   On land the fighting was between the
regular armies.   At sea privateers were let loose
out of French, Flemish, and Spanish ports.   Enter-
prising individuals took out letters of marque and
went cruising to take the chance of what they
could catch.   The Channel was the chief hunting-
ground, as being the highway between Spain
and the Low Countries.   The interval was short
between privateers and pirates.   Vessels of all
sorts passed into the business.   The Scilly Isles
became a pirate stronghold.   The creeks and
estuaries in Cork and Kerry furnished hiding-
places where the rovers could lie with security
and share their plunder with the Irish chiefs.
The disorder grew wilder when the divorce of
Catherine of Aragon made Henry into the public
enemy of Papal Europe.   English traders and
fishing-smacks were plundered and sunk.   Their

crews went armed to defend themselves, and from Thames mouth to Land's End the Channel became the scene of desperate fights. The type of vessel altered to suit the new conditions. Life depended on speed of sailing. The State Papers describe squadrons of French or Spaniards flying about, dashing into Dartmouth, Plymouth, or Falmouth, cutting out English coasters, or fighting one another.

After Henry was excommunicated, and Ireland rebelled, and England itself threatened disturbance, the King had to look to his security. He made little noise about it. But the Spanish ambassador reported him as silently building ships in the Thames and at Portsmouth. As invasion seemed imminent, he began with sweeping the seas of the looser vermin. A few swift well-armed cruisers pushed suddenly out of the Solent, caught and destroyed a pirate fleet in Mount's Bay, sent to the bottom some Flemish privateers in the Downs, and captured the Flemish admiral himself. Danger at home growing more menacing, and the monks spreading the fire which grew into the Pilgrimage of Grace, Henry suppressed the abbeys, sold the lands, and with the proceeds armed the coast with fortresses. 'You threaten me,' he seemed to say to them, 'that you will use the wealth our fathers gave you to overthrow my Government and bring in the invader. I will take your wealth, and I will use it to disappoint your treachery.' You may see the remnants of Henry's work in the fortresses anywhere along the coast from Berwick to the Land's End.

Louder thundered the Vatican. In 1539 Henry's time appeared to have come. France and Spain made peace, and the Pope's sentence was now expected to be executed by Charles or Francis, or both. A crowd of vessels large and small was collected in the Scheldt, for what purpose save to transport an army into England? Scotland had joined the Catholic League. Henry fearlessly appealed to the English people. Catholic peers and priests might conspire against him, but, explain it how we will, the nation was loyal to Henry and came to his side. The London merchants armed their ships in the river. From the seaports everywhere came armed brigantines and sloops. The fishermen of the West left their boats and nets to their wives, and the fishing was none the worse, for the women handled oar and sail and line and went to the whiting-grounds, while their husbands had gone to fight for their King. Genius kindled into discovery at the call of the country. Mr. Fletcher of Rye (be his name remembered) invented a boat the like of which was never seen before, which would work to windward, with sails trimmed fore and aft, the greatest revolution yet made in shipbuilding. A hundred and fifty sail collected at Sandwich to match the armament in the Scheldt; and Marillac, the French ambassador, reported with amazement the energy of King and people.

The Catholic Powers thought better of it. This was not the England which Reginald Pole had told them was longing for their appearance. The Scheldt force dispersed. Henry read Scotland a needed lesson. The Scots had thought to take him at disadvantage, and sit on his back when the Emperor attacked him. One morning when the people at Leith woke out of their sleep, they found an English fleet in the Roads; and before they had time to look about them, Leith was on

fire and Edinburgh was taken. Charles V., if he
had ever seriously thought of invading Henry,
returned to wiser counsels, and made an alliance
with him instead. The Pope turned to France.
If the Emperor forsook him, the Most Christian
King would help. He promised Francis that if he
could win England he might keep it for himself.
Francis resolved to try what he could do.

Five years had passed since the gathering
at Sandwich. It was now the summer of 1544.
The records say that the French collected at
Havre near 300 vessels, fighting ships, galleys,
and transports. Doubtless the numbers are far
exaggerated, but at any rate it was the largest
force ever yet got together to invade England,
capable, if well handled, of bringing Henry to his
knees. The plan was to seize and occupy the Isle
of Wight, destroy the English fleet, then take
Portsmouth and Southampton, and so advance
on London.

Henry's attention to his navy had not slackened.
He had built ship on ship. The *Great Harry* was
a thousand tons, carried 700 men, and was the
wonder of the day. There were a dozen others

scarcely less imposing. The King called again on
the nation, and again the nation answered. In
England altogether there were 150,000 men in
arms in field or garrison. In the King's fleet at
Portsmouth there were 12,000 seamen, and the
privateers of the West crowded up eagerly as
before. It is strange, with the notions which
we have allowed ourselves to form of Henry, to
observe the enthusiasm with which the whole
country, as yet undivided by doctrinal quarrels,
rallied a second time to defend him.

In this Portsmouth fleet lay undeveloped the
genius of the future naval greatness of England.
A small fact connected with it is worth recording.
The watchword on board was, 'God save the
King'; the answer was, 'Long to reign over us':
the earliest germ discoverable of the English
National Anthem.

The King had come himself to Portsmouth
to witness the expected attack. The fleet was
commanded by Lord Lisle, afterwards Duke of
Northumberland. It was the middle of July.
The French crossed from Havre unfought with,
and anchored in St. Helens Roads off Brading

Harbour. The English, being greatly inferior in
numbers, lay waiting for them inside the Spit.
The morning after the French came in was still
and sultry. The English could not move for
want of wind. The galleys crossed over and
engaged them for two or three hours with some
advantage. The breeze rose at noon; a few fast
sloops got under way and easily drove them back.
But the same breeze which enabled the English
to move brought a serious calamity with it. The
Mary Rose, one of Lisle's finest vessels, had been
under the fire of the galleys. Her ports had
been left open, and when the wind sprang up, she
heeled over, filled, and went down, carrying two
hundred men along with her. The French saw
her sink, and thought their own guns had done
it. They hoped to follow up their success. At
night they sent over boats to take soundings, and
discover the way into the harbour. The boats
reported that the sandbanks made the approach
impossible. The French had no clear plan of
action. They tried a landing in the island, but
the force was too small, and failed. They weighed
anchor and brought up again behind Selsea Bill,

where Lisle proposed to run them down in the dark, taking advantage of the tide. But they had an enemy to deal with worse than Lisle, on board their own ships, which explained their distracted movements. Hot weather, putrid meat, and putrid water had prostrated whole ships' companies with dysentery. After a three weeks' ineffectual cruise they had to hasten back to Havre, break up, and disperse. The first great armament which was to have recovered England to the Papacy had effected nothing. Henry had once more shown his strength, and was left undisputed master of the narrow seas.

So matters stood for what remained of Henry's reign. As far as he had gone, he had quarrelled with the Pope, and had brought the Church under the law. So far the country generally had gone with him, and there had been no violent changes in the administration of religion. When Henry died the Protector abolished the old creed, and created a new and perilous cleavage between Protestant and Catholic, and, while England needed the protection of a navy more than ever, allowed the fine fleet which Henry had left to fall

into decay. The spirit of enterprise grew with
the Reformation. Merchant companies opened
trade with Russia and the Levant; adventurous
sea captains went to Guinea for gold. Sir Hugh
Willoughby followed the phantom of the North-
west Passage, turning eastward round the North
Cape to look for it, and perished in the ice.
English commerce was beginning to grow in spite
of the Protector's experiments; but a new and
infinitely dangerous element had been introduced
by the change of religion into the relations of
English sailors with the Catholic Powers, and
especially with Spain. In their zeal to keep out
heresy, the Spanish Government placed their
harbours under the control of the Holy Office.
Any vessel in which an heretical book was found
was confiscated, and her crew carried to the
Inquisition prisons. It had begun in Henry's
time. The Inquisitors attempted to treat schism
as heresy and arrest Englishmen in their ports.
But Henry spoke up stoutly to Charles V., and
the Holy Office had been made to hold its hand.
All was altered now. It was not necessary that
a poor sailor should have been found teaching

heresy. It was enough if he had an English
Bible and Prayer Book with him in his kit; and
stories would come into Dartmouth or Plymouth
how some lad that everybody knew—Bill or Jack
or Tom, who had wife or father or mother among
them, perhaps—had been seized hold of for no
other crime, been flung into a dungeon, tortured,
starved, set to work in the galleys, or burned in
a fool's coat, as they called it, at an *auto da fé* at
Seville.

The object of the Inquisition was partly political: it was meant to embarrass trade and make
the people impatient of changes which produced
so much inconvenience. The effect was exactly
the opposite. Such accounts when brought home
created fury. There grew up in the seagoing
population an enthusiasm of hatred for that holy
institution, and a passionate desire for revenge.

The natural remedy would have been war;
but the division of nations was crossed by the
division of creeds; and each nation had allies in
the heart of every other. If England went to
war with Spain, Spain could encourage insurrection among the Catholics. If Spain or France

declared war against England, England could help the Huguenots or the Holland Calvinists. All Governments were afraid alike of a general war of religion which might shake Europe in pieces. Thus individuals were left to their natural impulses. The Holy Office burnt English or French Protestants wherever it could catch them. The Protestants revenged their injuries at their own risk and in their own way, and thus from Edward VI.'s time to the end of the century privateering came to be the special occupation of adventurous honourable gentlemen, who could serve God, their country, and themselves in fighting Catholics. Fleets of these dangerous vessels swept the Channel, lying in wait at Scilly, or even at the Azores—disowned in public by their own Governments while secretly countenanced, making war on their own account on what they called the enemies of God. In such a business, of course, there were many mere pirates engaged who cared neither for God nor man. But it was the Protestants who were specially impelled into it by the cruelties of the Inquisition. The Holy Office began the work with the *autos da fé*. The

privateers robbed, burnt, and scuttled Catholic
ships in retaliation. One fierce deed produced
another, till right and wrong were obscured in
the passion of religious hatred. Vivid pictures
of these wild doings survive in the English and
Spanish State Papers. Ireland was the rovers'
favourite haunt. In the universal anarchy there,
a little more or a little less did not signify.
Notorious pirate captains were to be met in Cork
or Kinsale, collecting stores, casting cannon, or
selling their prizes — men of all sorts, from
fanatical saints to undisguised ruffians. Here is
one incident out of many to show the heights to
which temper had risen.

'Long peace,' says someone, addressing the
Privy Council early in Elizabeth's time, 'becomes
by force of the Spanish Inquisition more hurtful
than open war. It is the secret, determined
policy of Spain to destroy the English fleet,
pilots, masters and sailors, by means of the
Inquisition. The Spanish King pretends he
dares not offend the Holy House, while we in
England say we may not proclaim war against
Spain in revenge of a few. Not long since the

Spanish Inquisition executed sixty persons of St. Malo, notwithstanding entreaty to the King of Spain to spare them. Whereupon the Frenchmen armed their pinnaces, lay for the Spaniards, took a hundred and beheaded them, sending the Spanish ships to the shore with their heads, leaving in each ship but one man to render the cause of the revenge. Since which time Spanish Inquisitors have never meddled with those of St. Malo.'

A colony of Huguenot refugees had settled on the coast of Florida. The Spaniards heard of it, came from St. Domingo, burnt the town, and hanged every man, woman, and child, leaving an inscription explaining that the poor creatures had been killed, not as Frenchmen, but as heretics. Domenique de Gourges, of Rochelle, heard of this fine exploit of fanaticism, equipped a ship, and sailed across. He caught the Spanish garrison which had been left in occupation and swung them on the same trees—with a second scroll saying that they were dangling there, not as Spaniards, but as murderers.

The genius of adventure tempted men of

highest birth into the rovers' ranks. Sir Thomas
Seymour, the Protector's brother and the King's
uncle, was Lord High Admiral. In his time of
office, complaints were made by foreign merchants
of ships and property seized at the Thames
mouth. No redress could be had; no restitution
made; no pirate was even punished, and Seymour's personal followers were seen suspiciously
decorated with Spanish ornaments. It appeared
at last that Seymour had himself bought the
Scilly Isles, and if he could not have his way at
Court, it was said that he meant to set up there
as a pirate chief.

The persecution under Mary brought in more
respectable recruits than Seymour. The younger
generation of the western families had grown
with the times. If they were not theologically
Protestant, they detested tyranny. They detested
the marriage with Philip, which threatened the
independence of England. At home they were
powerless, but the sons of honourable houses—
Strangways, Tremaynes, Staffords, Horseys,
Carews, Killegrews, and Cobhams—dashed out
upon the water to revenge the Smithfield mas-

sacres. They found help where it could least have been looked for. Henry II. of France hated heresy, but he hated Spain worse. Sooner than see England absorbed in the Spanish monarchy, he forgot his bigotry in his politics. He furnished these young mutineers with ships and money and letters of marque. The Huguenots were their natural friends. With Rochelle for an arsenal, they held the mouth of the Channel, and harassed the communications between Cadiz and Antwerp. It was a wild business: enterprise and buccaneering sanctified by religion and hatred of cruelty; but it was a school like no other for seamanship, and a school for the building of vessels which could outsail all others on the sea; a school, too, for the training up of hardy men, in whose blood ran detestation of the Inquisition and the Inquisition's master. Every other trade was swallowed up or coloured by privateering; the merchantmen went armed, ready for any work that offered; the Iceland fleet went no more in search of cod; the Channel boatmen forsook nets and lines and took to livelier occupations; Mary was too busy burning heretics to look to the police of the seas; her father's fine ships rotted in harbour; her father's coast-forts were deserted or dismantled; she lost Calais; she lost the hearts of her people in forcing them into orthodoxy; she left the seas to the privateers; and no trade flourished, save what the Catholic Powers called piracy.

When Elizabeth came to the throne, the whole merchant navy of England engaged in lawful commerce amounted to no more than 50,000 tons. You may see more now passing every day through the Gull Stream. In the service of the Crown there were but seven revenue cruisers in commission, the largest 120 tons, with eight merchant brigs altered for fighting. In harbour there were still a score of large ships, but they were dismantled and rotting; of artillery fit for sea work there was none. The men were not to be had, and, as Sir William Cecil said, to fit out ships without men was to set armour on stakes on the sea-shore. The mariners of England were otherwise engaged, and in a way which did not please Cecil. He was the ablest minister that Elizabeth had. He saw at once that on the navy the

prosperity and even the liberty of England must
eventually depend. If England were to remain
Protestant, it was not by articles of religion or
acts of uniformity that she could be saved without
a fleet at the back of them. But he was old-
fashioned. He believed in law and order, and he
has left a curious paper of reflections on the
situation. The ships' companies in Henry VIII.'s
days were recruited from the fishing-smacks, but
the Reformation itself had destroyed the fishing
trade. In old times, Cecil said, no flesh was
eaten on fish days. The King himself could
not have license. Now to eat beef or mutton on
fish days was the test of a true believer. The
English Iceland fishery used to supply Normandy
and Brittany as well as England. Now it had
passed to the French. The Chester men used to
fish the Irish seas. Now they had left them to
the Scots. The fishermen had taken to privateering because the fasts of the Church were neglected.
He saw it was so. He recorded his own opinion
that piracy, as he called it, was *detestable*, and
could not last. He was to find that it could last,
that it was to form the special discipline of the

generation whose business would be to fight the
Spaniards.   But he struggled hard against the
unwelcome conclusion.   He tried to revive lawful
trade by a Navigation Act.   He tried to restore
the fisheries by Act of Parliament.   He introduced
a Bill recommending godly abstinence as a means
to virtue, making the eating of meat on Fridays
and Saturdays a misdemeanour, and adding
Wednesday as a half fish-day.   The House of
Commons laughed at him as bringing back Popish
mummeries.   To please the Protestants he inserted
a clause, that the statute was politicly meant for
the increase of fishermen and mariners, not for
any superstition in the choice of meats; but it
was no use.   The Act was called in mockery
'Cecil's Fast,' and the recovery of the fisheries
had to wait till the natural inclination of human
stomachs for fresh whiting and salt cod should
revive of itself.

Events had to take their course.   Seamen
were duly provided in other ways, and such as
the time required.   Privateering suited Elizabeth's
convenience, and suited her disposition.   She liked
daring and adventure.   She liked men who would

do her work without being paid for it, men whom
she could disown when expedient; who would
understand her, and would not resent it. She
knew her turn was to come when Philip had
leisure to deal with her, if she could not secure
herself meanwhile. Time was wanted to restore
the navy. The privateers were a resource in the
interval. They might be called pirates while
there was formal peace. The name did not
signify. They were really the armed force of the
country. After the war broke out in the Netherlands, they had commissions from the Prince of
Orange. Such commissions would not save them
if taken by Spain, but it enabled them to sell
their prizes, and for the rest they trusted to their
speed and their guns. When Elizabeth was at
war with France about Havre, she took the most
noted of them into the service of the Crown. Ned
Horsey became Sir Edward and Governor of the
Isle of Wight; Strangways, a Red Rover in his
way, who had been the terror of the Spaniards,
was killed before Rouen; Tremayne fell at Havre,
mourned over by Elizabeth; and Champernowne,
one of the most gallant of the whole of them,

was killed afterwards at Coligny's side at Mon-
contour.

But others took their places: the wild hawks
as thick as seagulls flashing over the waves, fair
wind or foul, laughing at pursuit, brave, reckless,
devoted, the crews the strangest medley: English
from the Devonshire and Cornish creeks, Huguenots from Rochelle; Irish kernes with long
skenes, 'desperate, unruly persons with no kind
of mercy.'

The Holy Office meanwhile went on in cold,
savage resolution: the Holy Office which had
begun the business and was the cause of it.

A note in Cecil's hand says that in the one
year 1562 twenty-six English subjects had been
burnt at the stake in different parts of Spain.
Ten times as many were starving in Spanish
dungeons, from which occasionally, by happy
accident, a cry could be heard like this which
follows. In 1561 an English merchant writes
from the Canaries:

'I was taken by those of the Inquisition
twenty months past, put into a little dark house
two paces long, loaded with irons, without sight

D

of sun or moon all that time. When I was arraigned I was charged that I should say our mass was as good as theirs; that I said I would rather give money to the poor than buy Bulls of Rome with it. I was charged with being a subject to the Queen's grace, who, they said, was enemy to the Faith, Antichrist, with other opprobrious names; and I stood to the defence of the Queen's Majesty, proving the infamies most untrue. Then I was put into Little Ease again, protesting very innocent blood to be demanded against the judge before Christ.'

The innocent blood of these poor victims had not to wait to be avenged at the Judgment Day. The account was presented shortly and promptly at the cannon's mouth.

LECTURE II

JOHN HAWKINS AND THE AFRICAN SLAVE TRADE

I BEGIN this lecture with a petition addressed to Queen Elizabeth. Thomas Seely, a merchant of Bristol, hearing a Spaniard in a Spanish port utter foul and slanderous charges against the Queen's character, knocked him down. To knock a man down for telling lies about Elizabeth might be a breach of the peace, but it had not yet been declared heresy. The Holy Office, however, seized Seely, threw him into a dungeon, and kept him starving there for three years, at the end of which he contrived to make his condition known in England. The Queen wrote herself to Philip to protest. Philip would not interfere. Seely remained in prison and in irons, and the result was a petition from his wife, in which the temper which was rising can be read as in letters of fire.

Dorothy Seely demands that 'the friends of her Majesty's subjects so imprisoned and tormented in Spain may make out ships at their proper charges, take such Inquisitors or other Papistical subjects of the King of Spain as they can by sea or land, and retain them in prison with such torments and diet as her Majesty's subjects be kept with in Spain, and on complaint made by the King to give such answer as is now made when her Majesty sues for subjects imprisoned by the Inquisition. Or that a Commission be granted to the Archbishop of Canterbury and the other bishops word for word for foreign Papists as the Inquisitors have in Spain for the Protestants. So that all may know that her Majesty cannot and will not longer endure the spoils and torments of her subjects, and the Spaniards shall not think this noble realm dares not seek revenge of such importable wrongs.'

Elizabeth issued no such Commission as Dorothy Seely asked for, but she did leave her subjects to seek their revenge in their own way, and they sought it sometimes too rashly.

In the summer of 1563 eight English merchantmen anchored in the roads of Gibraltar. England and France were then at war. A French brig came in after them, and brought up near. At sea, if they could take her, she would have been a lawful prize. Spaniards under similar circumstances had not respected the neutrality of English harbours. The Englishmen were perhaps in doubt what to do, when the officers of the Holy Office came off to the French ship. The sight of the black familiars drove the English wild. Three of them made a dash at the French ship, intending to sink her. The Inquisitors sprang into their boat, and rowed for their lives. The castle guns opened, and the harbour police put out to interfere. The French ship, however, would have been taken, when unluckily Alvarez de Baçan, with a Spanish squadron, came round into the Straits. Resistance was impossible. The eight English ships were captured and carried off to Cadiz. The English flag was trailed under De Baçan's stern. The crews, two hundred and forty men in all, were promptly condemned to the galleys. In defence they could but say that the Frenchman was an enemy, and a moderate punishment would have sufficed for a violation of the harbour rules which the Spaniards themselves so little regarded. But the Inquisition was inexorable, and the men were treated with such peculiar brutality that after nine months ninety only of the two hundred and forty were alive.

Ferocity was answered by ferocity. Listen to this! The Cobhams of Cowling Castle were Protestants by descent. Lord Cobham was famous in the Lollard martyrology. Thomas Cobham, one of the family, had taken to the sea like many of his friends. While cruising in the Channel he caught sight of a Spaniard on the way from Antwerp to Cadiz with forty prisoners on board, consigned, it might be supposed, to the Inquisition. They were, of course, Inquisition prisoners; for other offenders would have been dealt with on the spot. Cobham chased her down into the Bay of Biscay, took her, scuttled her, and rescued the captives. But that was not enough. The captain and crew he sewed up in their own mainsail and flung them overboard. They were washed ashore dead, wrapped in their extraordinary winding-sheet. Cobham was called to account for this

exploit, but he does not seem to have been actually punished. In a very short time he was out
and away again at the old work. There were
plenty with him. After the business at Gibraltar,
Philip's subjects were not safe in English harbours.
Jacques le Clerc, a noted privateer, called Pie de
Palo from his wooden leg, chased a Spaniard into
Falmouth, and was allowed to take her under the
guns of Pendennis. The Governor of the castle
said that he could not interfere, because Le Clerc
had a commission from the Prince of Condé. It
was proved that in the summer of 1563 there
were 400 English and Huguenot rovers in and
about the Channel, and that they had taken 700
prizes between them. The Queen's own ships
followed suit. Captain Cotton in the *Phoenix*
captured an Antwerp merchantman in Flushing.
The harbour-master protested. Cotton laughed,
and sailed away with his prize. The Regent
Margaret wrote in indignation to Elizabeth. Such
insolence, she said, was not to be endured. She
would have Captain Cotton chastised as an example to all others. Elizabeth measured the
situation more correctly than the Regent; she

preferred to show Philip that she was not afraid
of him. She preferred to let her subjects discover for themselves that the terrible Spaniard
before whom the world trembled was but a
colossus stuffed with clouts. Until Philip consented to tie the hands of the Holy Office she did
not mean to prevent them from taking the law
into their own hands.

Now and then, if occasion required, Elizabeth
herself would do a little privateering on her own
account. In the next story that I have to tell
she appears as a principal, and her great minister,
Cecil, as an accomplice. The Duke of Alva had
succeeded Margaret as Regent of the Netherlands,
and was drowning heresy in its own blood. The
Prince of Orange was making a noble fight; but
all went ill with him. His troops were defeated, his
brother Louis was killed. He was still struggling,
helped by Elizabeth's money. But the odds
were terrible, and the only hope lay in the discontent of Alva's soldiers, who had not been paid
their wages, and would not fight without them.
Philip's finances were not flourishing, but he had
borrowed half a million ducats from a house at

Genoa for Alva's use. The money was to be delivered in bullion at Antwerp. The Channel privateers heard that it was coming and were on the look-out for it. The vessel in which it was sent took refuge in Plymouth, but found she had run into the enemy's nest. Nineteen or twenty Huguenot and English cruisers lay round her with commissions from Condé to take every Catholic ship they met with. Elizabeth's special friends thought and said freely that so rich a prize ought to fall to no one but her Majesty. Elizabeth thought the same, but for a more honourable reason. It was of the highest consequence that the money should not reach the Duke of Alva at that moment. Even Cecil said so, and sent the Prince of Orange word that it would be stopped in some way.

But how could it decently be done? Bishop Jewel relieved the Queen's mind (if it was ever disturbed) on the moral side of the question. The bishop held that it would be meritorious in a high degree to intercept a treasure which was to be used in the murder of Protestant Christians. But the how was the problem. To let the

privateers take it openly in Plymouth harbour
would, it was felt, be a scandal. Sir Arthur
Champernowne, the Vice-admiral of the West,
saw the difficulty and offered his services. He
had three vessels of his own in Condé's privateer
fleet, under his son Henry. As vice-admiral he
was first in command at Plymouth. He placed
a guard on board the treasure ship, telling the
captain it would be a discredit to the Queen's
Government if harm befell her in English waters.
He then wrote to Cecil.

'If,' he said, 'it shall seem good to your
honour that I with others shall give the attempt
for her Majesty's use which cannot be without
blood, I will not only take it in hand, but also
receive the blame thereof unto myself, to the end
so great a commodity should redound to her
Grace, hoping that, after bitter storms of her dis-
pleasure, showed at the first to colour the fact, I
shall find the calm of her favour in such sort as
I am most willing to hazard myself to serve her
Majesty. Great pity it were such a rich booty
should escape her Grace. But surely I am of that
mind that anything taken from that wicked nation

is both necessary and profitable to our commonwealth.'

Very shocking on Sir Arthur's part to write
such a letter: so many good people will think.   I
hope they will consider it equally shocking that
King Philip should have burned English sailors
at the stake because they were loyal to the laws
of their own country; that he was stirring war all
over Europe to please the Pope, and thrusting the
doctrines of the Council of Trent down the throats
of mankind at the sword's point.   Spain and
England might be at peace; Romanism and Protestantism were at deadly war, and war suspends
the obligations of ordinary life.   Crimes the most
horrible were held to be virtues in defence of the
Catholic faith.   The Catholics could not have the
advantage of such indulgences without the in-
conveniences.   The Protestant cause throughout
Europe was one, and assailed as the Protestants
were with such envenomed ferocity, they could
not afford to be nicely scrupulous in the means
they used to defend themselves.

Sir Arthur Champernowne was not called on
to sacrifice himself in such peculiar fashion, and a

better expedient was found to secure Alva's money.
The bullion was landed and was brought to London by road on the plea that the seas were unsafe.
It was carried to the Tower, and when it was once
inside the walls it was found to remain the property
of the Genoese until it was delivered at Antwerp.
The Genoese agent in London was as willing to
lend it to Elizabeth as to Philip, and indeed preferred the security. Elizabeth calmly said that
she had herself occasion for money, and would
accept their offer. Half of it was sent to the
Prince of Orange ; half was spent on the Queen's
navy.

Alva was of course violently angry. He arrested
every English ship in the Low Countries. He
arrested every Englishman that he could catch,
and sequestered all English property. Elizabeth
retaliated in kind. The Spanish and Flemish
property taken in England proved to be worth
double what had been secured by Alva. Philip
could not declare war. The Netherlands insurrection was straining his resources, and with Elizabeth
for an open enemy the whole weight of England
would have been thrown on the side of the Prince

of Orange. Elizabeth herself should have declared
war, people say, instead of condescending to
such tricks. Perhaps so; but also perhaps not.
These insults, steadily maintained and unresented,
shook the faith of mankind, and especially of her
own sailors, in the invincibility of the Spanish
colossus.

I am now to turn to another side of the
subject. The stories which I have told you
show the temper of the time, and the atmo-
sphere which men were breathing, but it will
be instructive to look more closely at individual
persons, and I will take first John Hawkins
(afterwards Sir John), a peculiarly characteristic
figure.

The Hawkinses of Plymouth were a solid
middle-class Devonshire family, who for two
generations had taken a leading part in the
business of the town. They still survive in the
county—Achins we used to call them before
school pronunciation came in, and so Philip wrote
the name when the famous John began to trouble
his dreams. I have already spoken of old William
Hawkins, John's father, whom Henry VIII. was

so fond of, and who brought over the Brazilian King. Old William had now retired and had left his place and his work to his son. John Hawkins may have been about thirty at Elizabeth's accession. He had witnessed the wild times of Edward VI. and Mary, but, though many of his friends had taken to the privateering business, Hawkins appears to have kept clear of it, and continued steadily at trade. One of these friends, and his contemporary, and in fact his near relation, was Thomas Stukely, afterwards so notorious—and a word may be said of Stukely's career as a contrast to that of Hawkins. He was a younger son of a leading county family, went to London to seek his fortune, and became a hanger-on of Sir Thomas Seymour. Doubtless he was connected with Seymour's pirating scheme at Scilly, and took to pirating as an occupation like other Western gentlemen. When Elizabeth became Queen, he introduced himself at Court and amused her with his conceit. He meant to be a king, nothing less than a king. He would go to Florida, found an empire there, and write to the Queen as his dearest sister. She gave him

leave to try.   He bought a vessel of 400 tons, got
100 tall soldiers to join him besides the crew, and
sailed from Plymouth in 1563.   Once out of
harbour, he announced that the sea was to be his
Florida.   He went back to the pirate business,
robbed freely, haunted Irish creeks, and set up
an intimacy with the Ulster hero, Shan O'Neil.
Shan and Stukely became bosom friends.   Shan
wrote to Elizabeth to recommend that she should
make over Ireland to Stukely and himself to
manage, and promised, if she agreed, to make it
such an Ireland as had never been seen, which
they probably would.   Elizabeth not consenting,
Stukely turned Papist, transferred his services to
the Pope and Philip, and was preparing a campaign in Ireland under the Pope's direction,
when he was tempted to join Sebastian of
Portugal in the African expedition, and there
got himself killed.

Stukely was a specimen of the foolish sort of
the young Devonshire men; Hawkins was exactly
his opposite.   He stuck to business, avoided
politics, traded with Spanish ports without offend-
ing the Holy Office, and formed intimacies and

connections with the Canary Islands especially,
where it was said 'he grew much in love and
favour with the people.'

At the Canaries he naturally heard much
about the West Indies. He was adventurous.
His Canaries friends told him that negroes were
great merchandise in the Spanish settlements in
Española, and he himself was intimately acquainted
with the Guinea coast, and knew how easily such
a cargo could be obtained.

We know to what the slave trade grew. We
have all learnt to repent of the share which England had in it, and to abhor everyone whose
hands were stained by contact with so accursed
a business. All that may be taken for granted;
but we must look at the matter as it would have
been represented at the Canaries to Hawkins
himself.

The Carib races whom the Spaniards found in
Cuba and St. Domingo had withered before them
as if struck by a blight. Many died under the
lash of the Spanish overseers; many, perhaps the
most, from the mysterious causes which have
made the presence of civilisation so fatal to the

Red Indian, the Australian, and the Maori. It is with men as it is with animals. The races which consent to be domesticated prosper and multiply. Those which cannot live without freedom pine like caged eagles or disappear like the buffaloes of the prairies.

Anyway, the natives perished out of the islands of the Caribbean Sea with a rapidity which startled the conquerors. The famous Bishop Las Casas pitied and tried to save the remnant that were left. The Spanish settlers required labourers for the plantations. On the continent of Africa were another race, savage in their natural state, which would domesticate like sheep and oxen, and learnt and improved in the white man's company. The negro never rose of himself out of barbarism; as his fathers were, so he remained from age to age; when left free, as in Liberia and in Hayti, he reverts to his original barbarism; while in subjection to the white man he showed then, and he has shown since, high capacities of intellect and character. Such is, such was the fact. It struck Las Casas that if negroes could be introduced into the West

E

Indian islands, the Indians might be left alone;
the negroes themselves would have a chance to
rise out of their wretchedness, could be made into
Christians, and could be saved at worst from the
horrid fate which awaited many of them in their
own country.

The black races varied like other animals:
some were gentle and timid, some were ferocious
as wolves. The strong tyrannised over the weak,
made slaves of their prisoners, occasionally ate
them, and those they did not eat they sacrificed
at what they called their *customs*—offered them
up and cut their throats at the altars of their
idols. These customs were the most sacred traditions of the negro race. They were suspended
while the slave trade gave the prisoners a value.
They revived when the slave trade was abolished.
When Lord Wolseley a few years back entered
Ashantee, the altars were coated thick with the
blood of hundreds of miserable beings who had
been freshly slaughtered there. Still later similar
horrid scenes were reported from Dahomey. Sir
Richard Burton, who was an old acquaintance
of mine, spent two months with the King of

Dahomey, and dilated to me on the benevolence and enlightenment of that excellent monarch. I asked why, if the King was so benevolent, he did not alter the customs. Burton looked at me with consternation. 'Alter the customs!' he said. 'Would you have the Archbishop of Canterbury alter the Liturgy?' Las Casas and those who thought as he did are not to be charged with infamous inhumanity if they proposed to buy these poor creatures from their captors, save them from Mumbo Jumbo, and carry them to countries where they would be valuable property, and be at least as well cared for as the mules and horses.

The experiment was tried and seemed to succeed. The negroes who were rescued from the customs and were carried to the Spanish islands proved docile and useful. Portuguese and Spanish factories were established on the coast of Guinea. The black chiefs were glad to make money out of their wretched victims, and readily sold them. The transport over the Atlantic became a regular branch of business. Strict laws were made for the good treatment of the

slaves on the plantations. The trade was carried
on under license from the Government, and an
import duty of thirty ducats per head was charged
on every negro that was landed. I call it an
experiment. The full consequences could not be
foreseen, and I cannot see that as an experiment
it merits the censures which in its later develop-
ments it eventually came to deserve. Las Casas,
who approved of it, was one of the most excellent
of men. Our own Bishop Butler could give no
decided opinion against negro slavery as it existed
in his time. It is absurd to say that ordinary
merchants and ship captains ought to have seen
the infamy of a practice which Las Casas advised
and Butler could not condemn. The Spanish and
Portuguese Governments claimed, as I said, the
control of the traffic. The Spanish settlers in
the West Indies objected to a restriction which
raised the price and shortened the supply. They
considered that having established themselves in
a new country they had a right to a voice in the
conditions of their occupancy. It was thus that
the Spaniards in the Canaries represented the
matter to John Hawkins. They told him that if

he liked to make the venture with a contraband cargo from Guinea, their countrymen would give him an enthusiastic welcome. It is evident from the story that neither he nor they expected that serious offence would be taken at Madrid. Hawkins at this time was entirely friendly with the Spaniards. It was enough if he could be assured that the colonists would be glad to deal with him.

I am not crediting him with the benevolent purposes of Las Casas. I do not suppose Hawkins thought much of saving black men's souls. He saw only an opportunity of extending his business among a people with whom he was already largely connected. The traffic was established. It had the sanction of the Church, and no objection had been raised to it anywhere on the score of morality. The only question which could have presented itself to Hawkins was of the right of the Spanish Government to prevent foreigners from getting a share of a lucrative trade against the wishes of its subjects. And his friends at the Canaries certainly did not lead him to expect any real opposition. One regrets that a famous Englishman should have been connected with the

slave trade; but we have no right to heap violent
censures upon him because he was no more
enlightened than the wisest of his contemporaries.

Thus, encouraged from Santa Cruz, Hawkins
on his return to England formed an African
company out of the leading citizens of London.
Three vessels were fitted out, Hawkins being
commander and part owner. The size of them
is remarkable: the *Solomon,* as the largest was
called, 120 tons; the *Swallow,* 100 tons; the
Jonas not above 40 tons. This represents them
as inconceivably small. They carried between
them a hundred men, and ample room had to be
provided besides for the blacks. There may have
been a difference in the measurement of tonnage.
We ourselves have five standards: builder's
measurement, yacht measurement, displacement,
sail area, and register measurement. Registered
tonnage is far under the others: a yacht registered
120 tons would be called 200 in a shipping list.
However that be, the brigantines and sloops
used by the Elizabethans on all adventurous
expeditions were mere boats compared with what
we should use now on such occasions. The reason

was obvious. Success depended on speed and sailing power. The art of building big square-rigged ships which would work to windward had not been yet discovered, even by Mr. Fletcher of Rye. The fore-and-aft rig alone would enable a vessel to tack, as it is called, and this could only be used with craft of moderate tonnage.

The expedition sailed in October 1562. They called at the Canaries, where they were warmly entertained. They went on to Sierra Leone, where they collected 300 negroes. They avoided the Government factories, and picked them up as they could, some by force, some by negotiation with local chiefs, who were as ready to sell their subjects as Sancho Panza intended to be when he got his island. They crossed without misadventure to St. Domingo, where Hawkins represented that he was on a voyage of discovery; that he had been driven out of his course and wanted food and money. He said he had certain slaves with him, which he asked permission to sell. What he had heard at the Canaries turned out to be exactly true. So far as the Governor of St. Domingo knew, Spain and England were at

peace. Privateers had not troubled the peace of
the Caribbean Sea, or dangerous heretics menaced
the Catholic faith there. Inquisitors might have
been suspicious, but the Inquisition had not yet
been established beyond the Atlantic. The Queen
of England was his sovereign's sister-in-law, and
the Governor saw no reason why he should con-
strue his general instructions too literally. The
planters were eager to buy, and he did not wish
to be unpopular. He allowed Hawkins to sell
two out of his three hundred negroes, leaving the
remaining hundred as a deposit should question
be raised about the duty. Evidently the only
doubt in the Governor's mind was whether the
Madrid authorities would charge foreign importers
on a higher scale. The question was new. No
stranger had as yet attempted to trade there.

Everyone was satisfied, except the negroes,
who were not asked their opinion. The profits
were enormous. A ship in the harbour was
about to sail for Cadiz. Hawkins invested most
of what he had made in a cargo of hides, for
which, as he understood, there was a demand in
Spain, and he sent them over in her in charge of

one of his partners. The Governor gave him a
testimonial for good conduct during his stay in
the port, and with this and with his three vessels
he returned leisurely to England, having, as he
imagined, been splendidly successful.

He was to be unpleasantly undeceived. A few
days after he had arrived at Plymouth, he met
the man whom he had sent to Cadiz with the
hides forlorn and empty-handed. The Inquisition,
he said, had seized the cargo and confiscated it.
An order had been sent to St. Domingo to forfeit
the reserved slaves. He himself had escaped for
his life, as the familiars had been after him.

Nothing shows more clearly how little thought
there had been in Hawkins that his voyage would
have given offence in Spain than the astonishment
with which he heard the news. He protested.
He wrote to Philip. Finding entreaties useless,
he swore vengeance; but threats were equally
ineffectual. Not a hide, not a farthing could he
recover. The Spanish Government, terrified at
the intrusion of English adventurers into their
western paradise to endanger the gold fleets, or
worse to endanger the purity of the faith, issued

orders more peremptory than ever to close the
ports there against all foreigners. Philip personally warned Sir Thomas Chaloner, the English
ambassador, that if such visits were repeated,
mischief would come of it. And Cecil, who
disliked all such semi-piratical enterprises, and
Chaloner, who was half a Spaniard and an old
companion in arms of Charles V., entreated their
mistress to forbid them.

Elizabeth, however, had her own views in such
matters. She liked money. She liked encouraging the adventurous disposition of her subjects,
who were fighting the State's battles at their
own risk and cost. She saw in Philip's anger a
confession that the West Indies was his vulnerable point; and that if she wished to frighten
him into letting her alone, and to keep the
Inquisition from burning her sailors, there was
the place where Philip would be more sensitive.
Probably, too, she thought that Hawkins had
done nothing for which he could be justly
blamed. He had traded at St. Domingo with
the Governor's consent, and confiscation was
sharp practice.

This was clearly Hawkins's own view of the matter. He had injured no one. He had offended no pious ears by parading his Protestantism. He was not Philip's subject, and was not to be expected to know the instructions given by the Spanish Government in the remote corners of their dominions. If anyone was to be punished, it was not he but the Governor. He held that he had been robbed, and had a right to indemnify himself at the King's expense. He would go out again. He was certain of a cordial reception from the planters. Between him and them there was the friendliest understanding. His quarrel was with Philip, and Philip only. He meant to sell a fresh cargo of negroes, and the Madrid Government should go without their 30 per cent. duty.

Elizabeth approved. Hawkins had opened the road to the West Indies. He had shown how easy slave smuggling was, and how profitable it was; how it was also possible for the English to establish friendly relations with the Spanish settlers in the West Indies, whether Philip liked it or not. Another company was formed for a

second trial. Elizabeth took shares, Lord Pem-
broke took shares, and other members of the
Council. The Queen lent the *Jesus*, a large ship
of her own, of 700 tons. Formal instructions
were given that no wrong was to be done to the
King of Spain, but what wrong might mean was
left to the discretion of the commander. Where
the planters were all eager to purchase, means of
traffic would be discovered without collision with
the authorities. This time the expedition was to
be on a larger scale, and a hundred soldiers were
put on board to provide for contingencies. Thus
furnished, Hawkins started on his second voyage
in October 1564. The autumn was chosen, to
avoid the extreme tropical heats. He touched
as before to see his friends at the Canaries. He
went on to the Rio Grande, met with adventures
bad and good, found a chief at war with a neighbouring tribe, helped to capture a town and take
prisoners, made purchases at a Portuguese factory.
In this way he now secured 400 human cattle,
perhaps for a better fate than they would have
met with at home, and with these he sailed off in
the old direction. Near the equator he fell in

with calms; he was short of water, and feared to
lose some of them; but, as the record of the
voyage puts it, 'Almighty God would not suffer
His elect to perish,' and sent a breeze which
carried him safe to Dominica. In that wettest
of islands he found water in plenty, and had then
to consider what next he would do. St. Domingo,
he thought, would be no longer safe for him; so
he struck across to the Spanish Main to a place
called Burboroata, where he might hope that
nothing would be known about him. In this he
was mistaken. Philip's orders had arrived: no
Englishman of any creed or kind was to be
allowed to trade in his West India dominions.
The settlers, however, intended to trade. They
required only a display of force that they might
pretend that they were yielding to compulsion.
Hawkins told his old story. He said that he was
out on the service of the Queen of England. He
had been driven off his course by bad weather.
He was short of supplies and had many men
on board, who might do the town some mischief
if they were not allowed to land peaceably and
buy and sell what they wanted. The Governor

affecting to hesitate, he threw 120 men on shore, and brought his guns to bear on the castle. The Governor gave way under protest. Hawkins was to be permitted to sell half his negroes. He said that as he had been treated so inhospitably he would not pay the 30 per cent. The King of Spain should have $7\frac{1}{2}$, and no more. The settlers had no objection. The price would be the less, and with this deduction his business was easily finished off. He bought no more hides, and was paid in solid silver.

From Burboroata he went on to Rio de la Hacha, where the same scene was repeated. The whole 400 were disposed of, this time with ease and complete success. He had been rapid, and had the season still before him. Having finished his business, he surveyed a large part of the Caribbean Sea, taking soundings, noting the currents, and making charts of the coasts and islands. This done, he turned homewards, following the east shore of North America as far as Newfoundland. There he gave his crew a change of diet, with fresh cod from the Banks, and after eleven months' absence he sailed into Padstow, having lost but twenty men in the whole adventure, and bringing back 60 per cent. to the Queen and the other shareholders.

Nothing succeeds like success. Hawkins's praises were in everyone's mouth, and in London he was the hero of the hour. Elizabeth received him at the palace. The Spanish ambassador, De Silva, met him there at dinner. He talked freely of where he had been and of what he had done, only keeping back the gentle violence which he had used. He regarded this as a mere farce, since there had been no one hurt on either side. He boasted of having given the greatest satisfaction to the Spaniards who had dealt with him. De Silva could but bow, report to his master, and ask instructions how he was to proceed.

Philip was frightfully disturbed. He saw in prospect his western subjects allying themselves with the English — heresy creeping in among them; his gold fleets in danger, all the possibilities with which Elizabeth had wished to alarm him. He read and re-read De Silva's letters, and opposite the name of Achines he wrote startled interjections on the margin: ' Ojo ! Ojo !'

The political horizon was just then favourable to Elizabeth. The Queen of Scots was a prisoner in Loch Leven; the Netherlands were in revolt; the Huguenots were looking up in France; and when Hawkins proposed a third expedition, she thought that she could safely allow it. She gave him the use of the *Jesus* again, with another smaller ship of hers, the *Minion*. He had two of his own still fit for work; and a fifth, the *Judith*, was brought in by his young cousin, Francis Drake, who was now to make his first appearance on the stage. I shall tell you by-and-by who and what Drake was. Enough to say now that he was a relation of Hawkins, the owner of a small smart sloop or brigantine, and ambitious of a share in a stirring business.

The Plymouth seamen were falling into dangerous contempt of Philip. While the expedition was fitting out, a ship of the King's came into Catwater with more prisoners from Flanders. She was flying the Castilian flag, contrary to rule, it was said, in English harbours. The treatment of the English ensign at Gibraltar had not been forgiven, and Hawkins ordered the Spanish captain to strike his colours. The captain refused, and Hawkins instantly fired into him. In the confusion the prisoners escaped on board the *Jesus* and were let go. The captain sent a complaint to London, and Cecil—who disapproved of Hawkins and all his proceedings—sent down an officer to inquire into what had happened. Hawkins, confident in Elizabeth's protection, quietly answered that the Spaniard had broken the laws of the port, and that it was necessary to assert the Queen's authority.

'Your mariners,' said De Silva to her, 'rob our subjects on the sea, trade where they are forbidden to go, and fire upon our ships in your harbours. Your preachers insult my master from their pulpits, and when we remonstrate we are answered with menaces. We have borne so far with their injuries, attributing them rather to temper and bad manners than to deliberate purpose. But, seeing that no redress can be had, and that the same treatment of us continues, I must consult my Sovereign's pleasure. For the last time, I require your Majesty to punish this outrage at Plymouth and preserve the peace between the two realms.'

F

No remonstrance could seem more just till the other side was heard. The other side was that the Pope and the Catholic Powers were undertaking to force the Protestants of France and Flanders back under the Papacy with fire and sword. It was no secret that England's turn was to follow as soon as Philip's hands were free. Meanwhile he had been intriguing with the Queen of Scots; he had been encouraging Ireland in rebellion; he had been persecuting English merchants and seamen, starving them to death in the Inquisition dungeons, or burning them at the stake. The Smithfield infamies were fresh in Protestant memories, and who could tell how soon the horrid work would begin again at home, if the Catholic Powers could have their way ?

If the King of Spain and his Holiness at Rome would have allowed other nations to think and make laws for themselves, pirates and privateers would have disappeared off the ocean. The West Indies would have been left undisturbed, and Spanish, English, French, and Flemings would have lived peacefully side by side as they do now. But spiritual tyranny had not yet learned its lesson, and the 'Beggars of the Sea' were to be Philip's schoolmasters in irregular but effective fashion.

Elizabeth listened politely to what De Silva said, promised to examine into his complaints, and allowed Hawkins to sail.

What befell him you will hear in the next lecture.

LECTURE III

SIR JOHN HAWKINS AND PHILIP THE SECOND

MY last lecture left Hawkins preparing to start on his third and, as it proved, most eventful voyage. I mentioned that he was joined by a young relation, of whom I must say a few preliminary words. Francis Drake was a Devonshire man, like Hawkins himself and Raleigh and Davis and Gilbert, and many other famous men of those days. He was born at Tavistock somewhere about 1540. He told Camden that he was of mean extraction. He meant merely that he was proud of his parents and made no idle pretensions to noble birth. His father was a tenant of the Earl of Bedford, and must have stood well with him, for Francis Russell, the heir of the earldom, was the boy's godfather. From him Drake took his Christian name. The Drakes

were early converts to Protestantism. Trouble
rising at Tavistock on the Six Articles Bill, they
removed to Kent, where the father, probably
through Lord Bedford's influence, was appointed
a lay chaplain in Henry VIII.'s fleet at Chatham.
In the next reign, when the Protestants were
uppermost, he was ordained and became vicar of
Upnor on the Medway. Young Francis took
early to the water, and made acquaintance with a
ship-master trading to the Channel ports, who
took him on board his ship and bred him as a
sailor. The boy distinguished himself, and his
patron when he died left Drake his vessel in his
will. For several years Drake stuck steadily to
his coasting work, made money, and made a solid
reputation. His ambition grew with his success.
The seagoing English were all full of Hawkins
and his West Indian exploits. The Hawkinses and
the Drakes were near relations. Hearing that
there was to be another expedition, and having
obtained his cousin's consent, Francis Drake sold
his brig, bought the *Judith*, a handier and faster
vessel, and with a few stout sailors from the
river went down to Plymouth and joined.

De Silva had sent word to Philip that
Hawkins was again going out, and preparations
had been made to receive him. Suspecting
nothing, Hawkins with his four consorts sailed, as
before, in October 1567. The start was ominous.
He was caught and badly knocked about by an
equinoctial in the Bay of Biscay. He lost his
boats. The *Jesus* strained her timbers and
leaked, and he so little liked the look of things
that he even thought of turning back and
giving up the expedition for the season. However, the weather mended. They put themselves
to rights at the Canaries, picked up their spirits,
and proceeded. The slave-catching was managed
successfully, though with some increased difficulty.
The cargo with equal success was disposed of at
the Spanish settlements. At one place the
planters came off in their boats at night to buy.
At Rio de la Hacha, where the most imperative
orders had been sent to forbid his admittance,
Hawkins landed a force as before and took
possession of the town, of course with the con-
nivance of the settlers. At Carthagena he was
similarly ordered off, and as Carthagena was

strongly fortified he did not venture to meddle with it. But elsewhere he found ample markets for his wares. He sold all his blacks. By this and by other dealings he had collected what is described as a vast treasure of gold, silver, and jewels. The hurricane season was approaching, and he made the best of his way homewards with his spoils, in the fear of being overtaken by it. Unluckily for him, he had lingered too long. He had passed the west point of Cuba and was working up the back of the island when a hurricane came down on him. The gale lasted four days. The ships' bottoms were foul and they could make no way. Spars were lost and rigging carried away. The *Jesus*, which had not been seaworthy all along, leaked worse than ever and lost her rudder. Hawkins looked for some port in Florida, but found the coast shallow and dangerous, and was at last obliged to run for San Juan de Ulloa, at the bottom of the Gulf of Mexico.

San Juan de Ulloa is a few miles only from Vera Cruz. It was at that time the chief port of Mexico, through which all the traffic passed

between the colony and the mother-country, and
was thus a place of some consequence. It stands
on a small bay facing towards the north. Across
the mouth of this bay lies a narrow ridge of sand
and shingle, half a mile long, which acts as a
natural breakwater and forms the harbour. This
ridge, or island as it was called, was uninhabited,
but it had been faced on the inner front by a
wall. The water was deep alongside, and vessels
could thus lie in perfect security, secured by their
cables to rings let into the masonry.

The prevailing wind was from the north,
bringing in a heavy surf on the back of the
island. There was an opening at both ends, but
only one available for vessels of large draught.
In this the channel was narrow, and a battery
at the end of the breakwater would completely
command it. The town stood on the opposite
side of the bay.

Into a Spanish port thus constructed Hawkins
entered with his battered squadron on September
16, 1568. He could not have felt entirely easy.
But he probably thought that he had no ill-will
to fear from the inhabitants generally, and that

the Spanish authorities would not be strong enough to meddle with him. His ill star had brought him there at a time when Alvarez de Baçan, the same officer who had destroyed the English ships at Gibraltar, was daily expected from Spain—sent by Philip, as it proved, specially to look for him. Hawkins, when he appeared outside, had been mistaken for the Spanish admiral, and it was under this impression that he had been allowed to enter. The error was quickly discovered on both sides.

Though still ignorant that he was himself De Baçan's particular object, yet De Baçan was the last officer whom in his crippled condition he would have cared to encounter. Several Spanish merchantmen were in the port richly loaded: with these of course he did not meddle, though, if reinforced, they might perhaps meddle with him. As his best resource he despatched a courier on the instant to Mexico to inform the Viceroy of his arrival, to say that he had an English squadron with him; that he had been driven in by stress of weather and need of repairs; that the Queen was an ally of the King of Spain;

and that, as he understood a Spanish fleet was likely soon to arrive, he begged the Viceroy to make arrangements to prevent disputes.

As yet, as I said in the last lecture, there was no Inquisition in Mexico. It was established there three years later, for the special benefit of the English. But so far there was no ill-will towards the English—rather the contrary. Hawkins had hurt no one, and the negro trading had been eminently popular. The Viceroy might perhaps have connived at Hawkins's escape, but again by ill-fortune he was himself under orders of recall, and his successor was coming out in this particular fleet with De Baçan.

Had he been well disposed and free to act it would still have been too late, for the very next morning, September 17, De Baçan was off the harbour mouth with thirteen heavily-armed galleons and frigates. The smallest of them carried probably 200 men, and the odds were now tremendous. Hawkins's vessels lay ranged along the inner bank or wall of the island. He instantly occupied the island itself and mounted guns at the point covering the way in. He then sent a

boat off to De Baçan to say that he was an
Englishman, that he was in possession of the
port, and must forbid the entrance of the Spanish
fleet till he was assured that there was to be no
violence. It was a strong measure to shut a
Spanish admiral out of a Spanish port in a time
of profound peace. Still, the way in was difficult,
and could not be easily forced if resolutely
defended. The northerly wind was rising; if it
blew into a gale the Spaniards would be on a lee
shore. Under desperate circumstances, desperate
things will be done. Hawkins in his subsequent
report thus explains his dilemma:—

'I was in two difficulties. Either I must
keep them out of the port, which with God's
grace I could easily have done, in which case
with a northerly wind rising they would have
been wrecked, and I should have been answerable;
or I must risk their playing false, which on the
whole I preferred to do.'

The northerly gale it appears did not rise, or
the English commander might have preferred the
first alternative. Three days passed in negotiation. De Baçan and Don Enriquez, the new

Viceroy, were naturally anxious to get into shelter out of a dangerous position, and were equally desirous not to promise any more than was absolutely necessary. The final agreement was that De Baçan and the fleet should enter without opposition. Hawkins might stay till he had repaired his damages, and buy and sell what he wanted; and further, as long as they remained the English were to keep possession of the island. This article, Hawkins says, was long resisted, but was consented to at last. It was absolutely necessary, for with the island in their hands, the Spaniards had only to cut the English cables, and they would have driven ashore across the harbour.

The treaty so drawn was formally signed. Hostages were given on both sides, and De Baçan came in. The two fleets were moored as far apart from each other as the size of the port would allow. Courtesies were exchanged, and for two days all went well. It is likely that the Viceroy and the admiral did not at first know that it was the very man whom they had been sent out to sink or capture who was lying so close to them.

When they did know it they may have looked on
him as a pirate, with whom, as with heretics,
there was no need to keep faith. Anyway, the
rat was in the trap, and De Baçan did not mean
to let him out. The *Jesus* lay furthest in; the
Minion lay beyond her towards the entrance,
moored apparently to a ring on the quay, but free
to move; and the *Judith*, further out again,
moored in the same way. Nothing is said of the
two small vessels remaining.

De Baçan made his preparations silently,
covered by the town. He had men in abundance
ready to act where he should direct. On the
third day, the 20th of September, at noon, the
Minion's crew had gone to dinner, when they saw
a large hulk of 900 tons slowly towing up alongside of them. Not liking such a neighbour, they
had their cable ready to slip and began to set
their canvas. On a sudden shots and cries were
heard from the town. Parties of English who
were on land were set upon; many were killed;
the rest were seen flinging themselves into the
water and swimming off to the ships. At the
same instant the guns of the galleons and of the

shore batteries opened fire on the *Jesus* and her
consorts, and in the smoke and confusion 300
Spaniards swarmed out of the hulk and sprang on
the *Minion's* decks. The *Minion's* men instantly
cut them down or drove them overboard, hoisted
sail, and forced their way out of the harbour,
followed by the *Judith*. The *Jesus* was left alone,
unable to stir. She defended herself desperately.
In the many actions which were fought afterwards between the English and the Spaniards,
there was never any more gallant or more severe.
De Baçan's own ship was sunk and the vice-
admiral's was set on fire. The Spanish, having
an enormous advantage in numbers, were able
to land a force on the island, seize the English
battery there, cut down the gunners, and turn
the guns close at hand on the devoted *Jesus*.
Still she fought on, defeating every attempt to
board, till at length De Baçan sent down fire-
ships on her, and then the end came. All that
Hawkins had made by his voyage, money, bullion,
the ship herself, had to be left to their fate.
Hawkins himself with the survivors of the crew
took to their boats, dashed through the enemy,

who vainly tried to take them, and struggled out
after the *Minion* and the *Judith*. It speaks ill
for De Baçan that with so large a force at his
command, and in such a position, a single Englishman escaped to tell the story.

Even when outside Hawkins's situation was
still critical and might well be called desperate.
The *Judith* was but fifty tons; the *Minion* not
above a hundred. They were now crowded up
with men. They had little water on board, and
there had been no time to refill their store-chests,
or fit themselves for sea. Happily the weather
was moderate. If the wind had risen, nothing
could have saved them. They anchored two
miles off to put themselves in some sort of order.
The Spanish fleet did not venture to molest
further so desperate a foe. On Saturday the 25th
they set sail, scarcely knowing whither to turn.
To attempt an ocean voyage as they were would
be certain destruction, yet they could not trust
longer to De Baçan's cowardice or forbearance.
There was supposed to be a shelter of some kind
somewhere on the east side of the Gulf of Mexico,
where it was hoped they might obtain provisions.

They reached the place on October 8, but found nothing. English sailors have never been wanting in resolution. They knew that if they all remained on board every one of them must starve. A hundred volunteered to land and take their chance. The rest on short rations might hope to make their way home. The sacrifice was accepted. The hundred men were put on shore. They wandered for a few days in the woods, feeding on roots and berries, and shot at by the Indians. At length they reached a Spanish station. where they were taken and sent as prisoners to Mexico. There was, as I said, no Holy Office as yet in Mexico. The new Viceroy, though he had been in the fight at San Juan de Ulloa, was not implacable. They were treated at first with humanity; they were fed, clothed, taken care of, and then distributed among the plantations. Some were employed as overseers, some as mechanics. Others, who understood any kind of business, were allowed to settle in towns, make money, and even marry and establish themselves. Perhaps Philip heard of it, and was afraid that so many heretics might introduce the plague. The quiet time lasted three years; at the end of those years the Inquisitors arrived, and then, as if these poor men had been the special object of that delightful institution, they were hunted up, thrown into dungeons, examined on their faith, tortured, some burnt in an *auto da fé*, some lashed through the streets of Mexico naked on horseback and returned to their prisons. Those who did not die under this pious treatment were passed over to the Holy Office at Seville and were condemned to the galleys.

Here I leave them for the moment. We shall presently hear of them again in a very singular connection. The *Minion* and *Judith* meanwhile pursued their melancholy way. They parted company. The *Judith*, being the better sailer, arrived first, and reached Plymouth in December, torn and tattered. Drake rode off post immediately to carry the bad news to London. The *Minion's* fate was worse. She made her course through the Bahama Channel, her crew dying as if struck with a pestilence, till at last there were hardly men enough left to handle the sails. They fell too far south for England, and at length had

G

to put into Vigo, where their probable fate would
be a Spanish prison. Happily they found other
English vessels in the roads there. Fresh hands
were put on board, and fresh provisions. With
these supplies Hawkins reached Mount's Bay a
month later than the *Judith*, in January 1569.

Drake had told the story, and all England was
ringing with it. Englishmen always think their
own countrymen are in the right. The Spaniards,
already in evil odour with the seagoing population, were accused of abominable treachery. The
splendid fight which Hawkins had made raised him
into a national idol, and though he had suffered
financially, his loss was made up in reputation
and authority. Every privateer in the West was
eager to serve under the leadership of the hero of
San Juan de Ulloa. He speedily found himself
in command of a large irregular squadron, and
even Cecil recognised his consequence. His chief
and constant anxiety was for the comrades whom
he had left behind, and he talked of a new expedition to recover them, or revenge them if they
had been killed ; but all things had to wait. They
probably found means of communicating with

him, and as long as there was no Inquisition in Mexico, he may have learnt that there was no immediate occasion for action.

Elizabeth put a brave face on her disappointment. She knew that she was surrounded with treason, but she knew also that the boldest course was the safest. She had taken Alva's money, and was less than ever inclined to restore it. She had the best of the bargain in the arrest of the Spanish and English ships and cargoes. Alva would not encourage Philip to declare war with England till the Netherlands were completely reduced, and Philip, with his leaden foot (*pié de plomo*), always preferred patience and intrigue. Time and he and the Pope were three powers which in the end, he thought, would prove irresistible, and indeed it seemed, after Hawkins's return, as if Philip would turn out to be right. The presence of the Queen of Scots in England had set in flame the Catholic nobles. The wages of Alva's troops had been wrung somehow out of the wretched Provinces, and his supreme ability and inexorable resolution were steadily grinding down the revolt. Every port in Holland and

Zealand was in Alva's hands. Elizabeth's throne was undermined by the Ridolfi conspiracy, the most dangerous which she had ever had to encounter. The only Protestant fighting power left on the sea which could be entirely depended on was in the privateer fleet, sailing, most of them, under a commission from the Prince of Orange.

This fleet was the strangest phenomenon in naval history. It was half Dutch, half English, with a flavour of Huguenot, and was commanded by a Flemish noble, Count de la Mark. Its headquarters were in the Downs or Dover Roads, where it could watch the narrow seas, and seize every Spanish ship that passed which was not too strong to be meddled with. The cargoes taken were openly sold in Dover market. If the Spanish ambassador is to be believed in a complaint which he addressed to Cecil, Spanish gentlemen taken prisoners were set up to public auction there for the ransom which they would fetch, and were disposed of for one hundred pounds each. If Alva sent cruisers from Antwerp to burn them out, they retreated under the guns of Dover Castle. Roving squadrons of them flew down to the Spanish coasts, pillaged churches, carried off church plate, and the captains drank success to piracy at their banquets out of chalices. The Spanish merchants at last estimated the property destroyed at three million ducats, and they said that if their flag could no longer protect them, they must decline to make further contracts for the supply of the Netherlands army.

It was life or death to Elizabeth. The Ridolfi plot, an elaborate and far-reaching conspiracy to give her crown to Mary Stuart and to make away with heresy, was all but complete. The Pope and Philip had approved; Alva was to invade; the Duke of Norfolk was to head an insurrection in the Eastern Counties. Never had she been in greater danger. Elizabeth was herself to be murdered. The intention was known, but the particulars of the conspiracy had been kept so secret that she had not evidence enough to take measures to protect herself. The privateers at Dover were a sort of protection; they would at least make Alva's crossing more difficult; but the most pressing exigency was the discovery of the details of the treason. Nothing was to be gained by concession; the only salvation was in daring.

At Antwerp there was a certain Doctor Story, maintained by Alva there to keep a watch on English heretics. Story had been a persecutor under Mary, and had defended heretic burning in Elizabeth's first Parliament. He had refused the oath of allegiance, had left the country, and had taken to treason. Cecil wanted evidence, and this man he knew could give it. A pretended informer brought Story word that there was an English vessel in the Scheldt which he would find worth examining. Story was tempted on board. The hatches were closed over him. He was delivered two days after at the Tower, when his secrets were squeezed out of him by the rack and he was then hanged.

Something was learnt, but less still than Cecil needed to take measures to protect the Queen. And now once more, and in a new character, we are to meet John Hawkins. Three years had passed since the catastrophe at San Juan de Ulloa. He had learnt to his sorrow that his poor companions had fallen into the hands of the

Holy Office at last; had been burnt, lashed,
starved in dungeons or worked in chains in the
Seville yards; and his heart, not a very tender
one, bled at the thoughts of them. The finest
feature in the seamen of those days was their
devotion to one another. Hawkins determined
that, one way or other, these old comrades of his
should be rescued. Entreaties were useless ; force
was impossible. There might still be a chance
with cunning. He would risk anything, even the
loss of his soul, to save them.

De Silva had left England. The Spanish
ambassador was now Don Guerau or Gerald de
Espes, and to him had fallen the task of watching
and directing the conspiracy. Philip was to give
the signal, the Duke of Norfolk and other Catholic
peers were to rise and proclaim the Queen of
Scots. Success would depend on the extent of
the disaffection in England itself; and the ambassador's business was to welcome and encourage
all symptoms of discontent. Hawkins knew
generally what was going on, and he saw in it
an opportunity of approaching Philip on his weak
side. Having been so much in the Canaries, he

probably spoke Spanish fluently. He called on
Don Guerau, and with audacious coolness represented that he and many of his friends were dis-
satisfied with the Queen's service. He said he
had found her faithless and ungrateful, and he
and they would gladly transfer their allegiance
to the King of Spain, if the King of Spain would
receive them. For himself, he would undertake
to bring over the whole privateer fleet of the
West, and in return he asked for nothing but the
release of a few poor English seamen who were
in prison at Seville.

Don Guerau was full of the belief that the
whole nation was ready to rebel. He eagerly
swallowed the bait which Hawkins threw to him.
He wrote to Alva, he wrote to Philip's secretary,
Cayas, expatiating on the importance of securing
such an addition to their party. It was true, he
admitted, that Hawkins had been a pirate, but
piracy was a common fault of the English, and
no wonder when the Spaniards submitted to being
plundered so meekly; the man who was offering
his services was bold, resolute, capable, and had
great influence with the English sailors; he

strongly advised that such a recruit should be encouraged.

Alva would not listen. Philip, who shuddered at the very name of Hawkins, was incredulous. Don Guerau had to tell Sir John that the King at present declined his offer, but advised him to go himself to Madrid, or to send some confidential friend with assurances and explanations.

Another figure now enters on the scene, a George Fitzwilliam. I do not know who he was, or why Hawkins chose him for his purpose. The Duke of Feria was one of Philip's most trusted ministers. He had married an English lady who had been a maid of honour to Queen Mary. It is possible that Fitzwilliam had some acquaintance with her or with her family. At any rate, he went to the Spanish Court; he addressed himself to the Ferias; he won their confidence, and by their means was admitted to an interview with Philip. He represented Hawkins as a faithful Catholic who was indignant at the progress of heresy in England, who was eager to assist in the overthrow of Elizabeth and the elevation of the Queen of Scots, and was able and willing to carry

along with him the great Western privateer fleet,
which had become so dreadful to the Spanish
mind. Philip listened and was interested. It
was only natural, he thought, that heretics should
be robbers and pirates. If they could be recovered
to the Church, their bad habits would leave them.
The English navy was the most serious obstacle
to the intended invasion. Still, Hawkins! The
Achines of his nightmares! It could not be.
He asked Fitzwilliam if his friend was acquainted
with the Queen of Scots or the Duke of Norfolk.
Fitzwilliam was obliged to say that he was not.
The credentials of John Hawkins were his own
right hand. He was making the King a magnificent offer: nothing less than a squadron of the
finest ships in the world—not perhaps in the
best condition, he added, with cool British impu-
dence, owing to the Queen's parsimony, but
easily to be put in order again if the King would
pay the seamen's wages and advance some money
for repairs. The release of a few poor prisoners
was a small price to ask for such a service.

The King was still wary, watching the bait
like an old pike, but hesitating to seize it; but the

duke and duchess were willing to be themselves
securities for Fitzwilliam's faith, and Philip
promised at last that if Hawkins would send him
a letter of recommendation from the Queen of
Scots herself, he would then see what could be
done. The Ferias were dangerously enthusiastic.
They talked freely to Fitzwilliam of the Queen
of Scots and her prospects. They trusted him
with letters and presents to her which would
secure his admittance to her confidence. Hawkins
had sent him over for the single purpose of
cheating Philip into releasing his comrades from
the Inquisition; and he had been introduced to
secrets of high political moment; like Saul, the
son of Kish, he had gone to seek his father's asses
and he had found a kingdom. Fitzwilliam
hurried home with his letters and his news.
Things were now serious. Hawkins could act
no further on his own responsibility. He consulted Cecil. Cecil consulted the Queen, and it
was agreed that the practice, as it was called,
should be carried further. It might lead to the
discovery of the whole secret.

Very treacherous, think some good people.

Well, there are times when one admires even
treachery—

> nec lex est justior ulla
> Quam necis artifices arte perire sua.

King Philip was confessedly preparing to encourage an English subject in treason to his
sovereign. Was it so wrong to hoist the
engineer with his own petard ? Was it wrong
of Hamlet to finger the packet of Rosencrantz
and Guildenstern and rewrite his uncle's despatch ?
Let us have done with cant in these matters.
Mary Stuart was at Sheffield Castle in charge of
Lord Shrewsbury, and Fitzwilliam could not see
her without an order from the Crown. Shrewsbury, though loyal to Elizabeth, was notoriously
well inclined to Mary, and therefore could not be
taken into confidence. In writing to him Cecil
merely said that friends of Fitzwilliam's were in
prison in Spain; that if the Queen of Scots
would intercede for them, Philip might be induced
to let them go. He might therefore allow Fitzwilliam to have a private audience with that Queen.

Thus armed, Fitzwilliam went down to Sheffield.
He was introduced. He began with presenting

Mary with the letters and remembrances from the Ferias, which at once opened her heart. It was impossible for her to suspect a friend of the duke and duchess. She was delighted at receiving a visitor from the Court of Spain. She was prudent enough to avoid dangerous confidences, but she said she was always pleased when she could do a service to Englishmen, and with all her heart would intercede for the prisoners. She wrote to Philip, she wrote to the duke and duchess, and gave the letters to Fitzwilliam to deliver. He took them to London, called on Don Gerald, and told him of his success. Don Gerald also wrote to his master, wrote unguardedly, and also trusted Fitzwilliam with the despatch.

The various packets were taken first to Cecil, and were next shown to the Queen. They were then returned to Fitzwilliam, who once more went off with them to Madrid. If the letters produced the expected effect, Cecil calmly observed that divers commodities would ensue. English sailors would be released from the Inquisition and the galleys. The enemy's intentions would be discovered. If the King of Spain

could be induced to do as Fitzwilliam had
suggested, and assist in the repairs of the ships
at Plymouth, credit would be obtained for a sum
of money which could be employed to his own
detriment. If Alva attempted the projected
invasion, Hawkins might take the ships as if to
escort him, and then do some notable exploit in
mid-Channel.

You will observe the downright directness of
Cecil, Hawkins, and the other parties in the
matter. There is no wrapping up their intentions
in fine phrases, no parade of justification. They
went straight to their point. It was very
characteristic of Englishmen in those stern,
dangerous times. They looked facts in the face,
and did what fact required. All really happened
exactly as I have described it: the story is told
in letters and documents of the authenticity of
which there is not the smallest doubt.

We will follow Fitzwilliam. He arrived at
the Spanish Court at the moment when Ridolfi
had brought from Rome the Pope's blessing on
the conspiracy. The final touches were being
added by the Spanish Council of State. All was

hope; all was the credulity of enthusiasm! Mary Stuart's letter satisfied Philip. The prisoners were dismissed, each with ten dollars in his pocket. An agreement was formally drawn and signed in the Escurial in which Philip gave Hawkins a pardon for his misdemeanours in the West Indies, a patent for a Spanish peerage, and a letter of credit for 40,000*l.* to put the privateers in a condition to do service, and the money was actually paid by Philip's London agent. Admitted as he now was to full confidence, Fitzwilliam learnt all particulars of the great plot. The story reads like a chapter from *Monte Cristo* and yet it is literally true.

It ends with a letter which I will read to you, from Hawkins to Cecil:—

'My very good Lord,—It may please your Honour to be advertised that Fitzwilliam is returned from Spain, where his message was acceptably received, both by the King himself, the Duke of Feria, and others of the Privy Council. His despatch and answer were with great expedition and great countenance and

favour of the King.   The Articles are sent to the
Ambassador with orders also for the money to
be paid to me by him, for the enterprise to
proceed with all diligence.   The pretence is that
my powers should join with the Duke of Alva's
powers, which he doth secretly provide in Flanders,
as well as with powers which will come with the
Duke of Medina Celi out of Spain, and to invade
this realm and set up the Queen of Scots.   They
have practised with us for the burning of Her
Majesty's ships.   Therefore there should be some
good care had of them, but not as it may appear
that anything is discovered.   The King has sent
a ruby of good price to the Queen of Scots, with
letters also which in my judgment were good to
be delivered.   The letters be of no importance,
but his message by word is to comfort her, and
say that he hath now none other care but to
place her in her own.   It were good also that
Fitzwilliam may have access to the Queen of
Scots to render thanks for the delivery of the
prisoners who are now at liberty.   It will be a
very good colour for your Lordship to confer with
him more largely.

'I have sent your Lordship the copy of my pardon from the King of Spain, in the order and manner I have it, with my great titles and honours from the King, from which God deliver me. Their practices be very mischievous, and they be never idle; but God, I hope, will confound them and turn their devices on their own necks.

'Your Lordship's most faithfully to my power,

'JOHN HAWKINS.'

A few more words will conclude this curious episode. With the clue obtained by Fitzwilliam, and confessions twisted out of Story and other unwilling witnesses, the Ridolfi conspiracy was unravelled before it broke into act. Norfolk lost his head. The inferior miscreants were hanged. The Queen of Scots had a narrow escape, and the Parliament accentuated the Protestant character of the Church of England by embodying the Thirty-nine Articles in a statute. Alva, who distrusted Ridolfi from the first and disliked encouraging rebellion, refused to interest himself further in Anglo-Catholic plots. Elizabeth and Cecil could now breathe more freely, and read

H

Philip a lesson on the danger of plotting against the lives of sovereigns.

So long as England and Spain were nominally at peace, the presence of De la Mark and his privateers in the Downs was at least indecent. A committee of merchants at Bruges represented that their losses by it amounted (as I said) to three million ducats. Elizabeth, being now in comparative safety, affected to listen to remonstrances, and orders were sent down to De la Mark that he must prepare to leave. It is likely that both the Queen and he understood each other, and that De la Mark quite well knew where he was to go, and what he was to do.

Alva now held every fortress in the Low Countries, whether inland or on the coast. The people were crushed. The duke's great statue stood in the square at Antwerp as a symbol of the annihilation of the ancient liberties of the Provinces. By sea alone the Prince of Orange still continued the unequal struggle; but if he was to maintain himself as a sea power anywhere, he required a harbour of his own in his own country. Dover and the Thames had served for a time as a base of operations, but it could not last, and without a footing in Holland itself eventual success was impossible. All the Protestant world was interested in his fate, and De la Mark, with his miscellaneous gathering of Dutch, English, and Huguenot rovers, were ready for any desperate exploit.

The order was to leave Dover immediately, but it was not construed strictly. He lingered in the Downs for six weeks. At length, one morning at the end of March 1572, a Spanish convoy known to be richly loaded appeared in the Straits. De la Mark lifted anchor, darted out on it, seized two of the largest hulks, rifled them, flung their crews overboard, and chased the rest up Channel. A day or two after he suddenly showed himself off Brille, at the mouth of the Meuse. A boat was sent on shore with a note to the governor, demanding the instant surrender of the town to the admiral of the Prince of Orange. The inhabitants rose in enthusiasm; the garrison was small, and the governor was obliged to comply. De la Mark took possession. A few priests and monks attempted resistance, but were put down without difficulty, and the leaders killed. The churches were cleared of their idols, and the mass replaced by the Calvinistic service. Cannon and stores, furnished from London, were landed, and Brille was made impregnable before Alva had realised what had happened to him. He is said to have torn his beard for anger. Flushing followed suit. In a week or two all the strongest places on the coast had revolted, and the pirate fleet had laid the foundation of the great Dutch Republic, which at England's side was to strike out of Philip's hand the sceptre of the seas, and to save the Protestant religion.

We may think as we please of these Beggars of the Ocean, these Norse corsairs come to life again with the flavour of Genevan theology in them; but for daring, for ingenuity, for obstinate determination to be spiritually free or to die for it, the like of the Protestant privateers of the sixteenth century has been rarely met with in this world.

England rang with joy when the news came that Brille was taken. Church bells pealed, and bonfires blazed. Money poured across in streams.

Exiled families went back to their homes—which were to be their homes once more—and the Zealanders and Hollanders, entrenched among their ditches, prepared for an amphibious conflict with the greatest power then upon the earth

LECTURE IV

DRAKE'S VOYAGE ROUND THE WORLD

I SUPPOSE some persons present have heard
the name of Lope de Vega, the Spanish poet
of Philip II.'s time. Very few of you probably
know more of him than his name, and yet he
ought to have some interest for us, as he was
one of the many enthusiastic young Spaniards
who sailed in the Great Armada. He had been
disappointed in some love affair. He was an
earnest Catholic. He wanted distraction, and it
is needless to say that he found distraction
enough in the English Channel to put his love
troubles out of his mind. His adventures brought
before him with some vividness the character of
the nation with which his own country was then
in the death-grapple, especially the character of
the great English seaman to whom the Spaniards

universally attributed their defeat. Lope studied
the exploits of Francis Drake from his first
appearance to his end, and he celebrated those
exploits, as England herself has never yet thought
it worth her while to do, by making him the hero
of an epic poem. There are heroes and heroes.
Lope de Vega's epic is called 'The Dragontea.'
Drake himself is the dragon, the ancient serpent
of the Apocalypse. We English have been contented to allow Drake a certain qualified praise.
We admit that he was a bold, dexterous sailor,
that he did his country good service at the
Invasion. We allow that he was a famous
navigator, and sailed round the world, which no
one else had done before him. But—there is
always a but—of course he was a robber and a
corsair, and the only excuse for him is that he
was no worse than most of his contemporaries.
To Lope de Vega he was a great deal worse. He
was Satan himself, the incarnation of the Genius
of Evil, the arch-enemy of the Church of God.

It is worth while to look more particularly
at the figure of a man who appeared to the
Spaniards in such terrible proportions. I, for my

part, believe a time will come when we shall see better than we see now what the Reformation was, and what we owe to it, and these sea-captains of Elizabeth will then form the subject of a great English national epic as grand as the 'Odyssey.'

In my own poor way meanwhile I shall try in these lectures to draw you a sketch of Drake and his doings as they appear to myself. To-day I can but give you a part of the rich and varied story, but if all goes well I hope I may be able to continue it at a future time.

I have not yet done with Sir John Hawkins. We shall hear of him again. He became the manager of Elizabeth's dockyards. He it was who turned out the ships that fought Philip's fleet in the Channel in such condition that not a hull leaked, not a spar was sprung, not a rope parted at an unseasonable moment, and this at a minimum of cost. He served himself in the squadron which he had equipped. He was one of the small group of admirals who met that Sunday afternoon in the cabin of the ark *Raleigh* and sent the fire-ships down to stir Medina Sidonia out of his anchorage at Calais. He was a child of the sea, and at sea he died, sinking at last into his mother's arms. But of this hereafter. I must speak now of his still more illustrious kinsman, Francis Drake.

I told you the other day generally who Drake was and where he came from; how he went to sea as a boy, found favour with his master, became early an owner of his own ship, sticking steadily to trade. You hear nothing of him in connection with the Channel pirates. It was not till he was five-and-twenty that he was tempted by Hawkins into the negro-catching business, and of this one experiment was enough. He never tried it again.

The portraits of him vary very much, as indeed it is natural that they should, for most of those which pass for Drake were not meant for Drake at all. It is the fashion in this country, and a very bad fashion, when we find a remarkable portrait with no name authoritatively attached to it, to christen it at random after some eminent man, and there it remains to perplex or mislead.

The best likeness of Drake that I know is an engraving in Sir William Stirling-Maxwell's

collection of sixteenth-century notabilities, representing him, as a scroll says at the foot of the
plate, at the age of forty-three. The face is
round, the forehead broad and full, with the short
brown hair curling crisply on either side. The
eyebrows are highly arched, the eyes firm, clear,
and open. I cannot undertake for the colour, but
I should judge they would be dark grey, like an
eagle's. The nose is short and thick, the mouth
and chin hid by a heavy moustache on the upper
lip, and a close-clipped beard well spread over
chin and cheek. The expression is good-humoured,
but absolutely inflexible, not a weak line to be
seen. He was of middle height, powerfully built,
perhaps too powerfully for grace, unless the
quilted doublet in which the artist has dressed
him exaggerates his breadth.

I have seen another portrait of him, with
pretensions to authenticity, in which he appears
with a slighter figure, eyes dark, full, thoughtful,
and stern, a sailor's cord about his neck with a
whistle attached to it, and a ring into which a
thumb is carelessly thrust, the weight of the
arms resting on it, as if in a characteristic

attitude. Evidently this is a carefully drawn likeness of some remarkable seaman of the time. I should like to believe it to be Drake, but I can feel no certainty about it.

We left him returned home in the *Judith* from San Juan de Ulloa, a ruined man. He had never injured the Spaniards. He had gone out with his cousin merely to trade, and he had met with a hearty reception from the settlers wherever he had been. A Spanish admiral had treacherously set upon him and his kinsman, destroyed half their vessels, and robbed them of all that they had. They had left a hundred of their comrades behind them, for whose fate they might fear the worst. Drake thenceforth considered Spanish property as fair game till he had made up his own losses. He waited quietly for four years till he had re-established himself, and then prepared to try fortune again in a more daring form.

The ill-luck at San Juan de Ulloa had risen from loose tongues. There had been too much talk about it. Too many parties had been concerned. The Spanish Government had notice and were prepared. Drake determined to act for

himself, have no partners, and keep his own
secret. He found friends to trust him with
money without asking for explanations. The
Plymouth sailors were eager to take their chance
with him. His force was absurdly small : a sloop
or brigantine of a hundred tons, which he called
the *Dragon* (perhaps, like Lope de Vega, playing
on his own name), and two small pinnaces. With
these he left Plymouth in the fall of the summer
of 1572. He had ascertained that Philip's gold
and silver from the Peruvian mines was landed
at Panama, carried across the isthmus on mules'
backs on the line of M. de Lesseps' canal, and
re-shipped at Nombre de Dios, at the mouth of
the Chagre River.

He told no one where he was going. He was
no more communicative than necessary after his
return, and the results, rather than the particulars,
of his adventure are all that can be certainly
known. Discretion told him to keep his counsel,
and he kept it.

The Drake family published an account of
this voyage in the middle of the next century,
but obviously mythical, in parts demonstrably

false, and nowhere to be depended on. It can be made out, however, that he did go to Nombre de Dios, that he found his way into the town, and saw stores of bullion there which he would have liked to carry off but could not. A romantic story of a fight in the town I disbelieve, first because his numbers were so small that to try force would have been absurd, and next because if there had been really anything like a battle an alarm would have been raised in the neighbourhood, and it is evident that no alarm was given. In the woods were parties of runaway slaves, who were called Cimarons. It was to these that Drake addressed himself, and they volunteered to guide him where he could surprise the treasure convoy on the way from Panama. His movements were silent and rapid. One interesting incident is mentioned which is authentic. The Cimarons took him through the forest to the watershed from which the streams flow to both oceans. Nothing could be seen through the jungle of undergrowth; but Drake climbed a tall tree, saw from the top of it the Pacific glittering below him, and made a vow that one day he would himself sail a ship in those waters.

For the present he had immediate work on hand. His guides kept their word. They led him to the track from Panama, and he had not long to wait before the tinkling was heard of the mule bells as they were coming up the pass. There was no suspicion of danger, not the faintest. The mule train had but its ordinary guard, who fled at the first surprise. The immense booty fell all into Drake's hands—gold, jewels, silver bars— and got with much ease, as Prince Hal said at Gadshill. The silver they buried, as too heavy for transport. The gold, pearls, rubies, emeralds, and diamonds they carried down straight to their ship. The voyage home went prosperously. The spoils were shared among the adventurers, and they had no reason to complain. They were wise enough to hold their tongues, and Drake was in a condition to look about him and prepare for bigger enterprises.

Rumours got abroad, spite of reticence. Imagination was high in flight just then; rash amateurs thought they could make their fortunes

in the same way, and tried it, to their sorrow.
A sort of inflation can be traced in English
sailors' minds as their work expanded.   Even
Hawkins—the clear, practical Hawkins—was infected.   This was not in Drake's line.   He kept
to prose and fact.   He studied the globe.   He
examined all the charts that he could get.   He
became known to the Privy Council and the
Queen, and prepared for an enterprise which would
make his name and frighten Philip in earnest.

The ships which the Spaniards used on the
Pacific were usually built on the spot.   But Magellan was known to have gone by the Horn, and
where a Portuguese could go an Englishman could
go.   Drake proposed to try.   There was a party in
Elizabeth's Council against these adventures, and
in favour of peace with Spain; but Elizabeth
herself was always for enterprises of pith and
moment.   She was willing to help, and others
of her Council were willing too, provided their
names were not to appear.   The responsibility
was to be Drake's own.   Again the vessels in
which he was preparing to tempt fortune seem
preposterously small.   The *Pelican*, or *Golden*

Hinde, which belonged to Drake himself, was called but 120 tons, at best no larger than a modern racing yawl, though perhaps no racing yawl ever left White's yard better found for the work which she had to do. The next, the *Elizabeth*, of London, was said to be eighty tons; a small pinnace of twelve tons, in which we should hardly risk a summer cruise round the Land's End, with two sloops or frigates of fifty and thirty tons, made the rest. The *Elizabeth* was commanded by Captain Winter, a Queen's officer, and perhaps a son of the old admiral.

We may credit Drake with knowing what he was about. He and his comrades were carrying their lives in their hands. If they were taken they would be inevitably hanged. Their safety depended on speed of sailing, and specially on the power of working fast to windward, which the heavy square-rigged ships could not do. The crews all told were 160 men and boys. Drake had his brother John with him. Among his officers were the chaplain, Mr. Fletcher, another minister of some kind who spoke Spanish, and in one of the sloops a mysterious Mr. Doughty.

Who Mr. Doughty was, and why he was sent out,
is uncertain.   When an expedition of consequence
was on hand, the Spanish party in the Cabinet
usually attached to it some second in command
whose business was to defeat the object.   When
Drake went to Cadiz in after years to singe King
Philip's beard, he had a colleague sent with him
whom he had to lock into his cabin before he
could get to his work.   So far as I can make out,
Mr. Doughty had a similar commission.   On this
occasion secrecy was impossible.   It was generally known that Drake was going to the Pacific
through Magellan Straits, to act afterwards on
his own judgment.   The Spanish ambassador,
now Don Bernardino de Mendoza, in informing
Philip of what was intended, advised him to send
out orders for the instant sinking of every English
ship, and the execution of every English sailor,
that appeared on either side the isthmus in West
Indian waters.   The orders were despatched, but
so impossible it seemed that an English pirate
could reach the Pacific, that the attention was
confined to the Caribbean Sea, and not a hint of
alarm was sent across to the other side.

I

On November 15, 1577, the *Pelican* and her consort sailed out of Plymouth Sound. The elements frowned on their start. On the second day they were caught in a winter gale. The *Pelican* sprung her mainmast, and they put back to refit and repair. But Drake defied auguries. Before the middle of December all was again in order. The weather mended, and with a fair wind and smooth water they made a fast run across the Bay of Biscay and down the coast to the Cape de Verde Islands. There taking up the north-east trades, they struck across the Atlantic, crossed the line, and made the South American continent in latitude 33° South. They passed the mouth of the Plate River, finding to their astonishment fresh water at the ship's side in fifty-four fathoms. All seemed so far going well, when one morning Mr. Doughty's sloop was missing, and he along with her. Drake, it seemed, had already reason to distrust Doughty, and guessed the direction in which he had gone. The *Marigold* was sent in pursuit, and he was overtaken and brought back. To prevent a repetition of such a performance, Drake took the

sloop's stores out of her, burnt her, distributed
the crew through the other vessels, and took Mr.
Doughty under his own charge. On June 20
they reached Port St. Julian, on the coast of
Patagonia. They had been long on the way, and
the southern winter had come round, and they
had to delay further to make more particular
inquiry into Doughty's desertion. An ominous
and strange spectacle met their eyes as they
entered the harbour. In that utterly desolate
spot a skeleton was hanging on a gallows, the
bones picked clean by the vultures. It was one
of Magellan's crew who had been executed there
for mutiny fifty years before. The same fate was
to befall the unhappy Englishman who had been
guilty of the same fault. Without the strictest
discipline it was impossible for the enterprise to
succeed, and Doughty had been guilty of worse
than disobedience. We are told briefly that his
conduct was found tending to contention, and
threatening the success of the voyage. Part he
was said to have confessed; part was proved
against him—one knows not what. A court was
formed out of the crew. He was tried, as near as

circumstances allowed, according to English usage.
He was found guilty, and was sentenced to die.
He made no complaint, or none of which a record
is preserved. He asked for the Sacrament, which
was of course allowed, and Drake himself communicated with him. They then kissed each
other, and the unlucky wretch took leave of his
comrades, laid his head on the block, and so
ended. His offence can be only guessed; but the
suspicious curiosity about his fate which was
shown afterwards by Mendoza makes it likely
that he was in Spanish pay. The ambassador
cross-questioned Captain Winter very particularly
about him, and we learn one remarkable fact from
Mendoza's letters not mentioned by any English
writer, that Drake was himself the executioner,
choosing to bear the entire responsibility.

'This done,' writes an eye-witness, ' the general
made divers speeches to the whole company, per-
suading us to unity, obedience, and regard of our
voyage, and for the better confirmation thereof
willed every man the Sunday following to prepare
himself to receive the Communion as Christian
brothers and friends ought to do, which was done

in very reverend sort; and so with good content-
ment every man went about his business.'

You must take this last incident into your
conception of Drake's character, think of it how
you please.

It was now midwinter, the stormiest season of
the year, and they remained for six weeks in Port
St. Julian. They burnt the twelve-ton pinnace,
as too small for the work they had now before
them, and there remained only the *Pelican*, the
Elizabeth, and the *Marigold*. In cold wild weather
they weighed at last, and on August 20 made the
opening of Magellan's Straits. The passage is
seventy miles long, tortuous and dangerous.
They had no charts. The ships' boats led, taking
soundings as they advanced. Icy mountains
overhung them on either side; heavy snow fell
below. They brought up occasionally at an
island to rest the men, and let them kill a few
seals and penguins to give them fresh food.
Everything they saw was new, wild, and wonderful.

Having to feel their way, they were three
weeks in getting through. They had counted on
reaching the Pacific that the worst of their work

was over, and that they could run north at once
into warmer and calmer latitudes. The peaceful
ocean, when they entered it, proved the stormiest
they had ever sailed on. A fierce westerly gale
drove them 600 miles to the south-east outside
the Horn. It had been supposed, hitherto, that
Tierra del Fuego was solid land to the South
Pole, and that the Straits were the only com-
munication between the Atlantic and the Pacific.
They now learnt the true shape and character of
the Western Continent. In the latitude of Cape
Horn a westerly gale blows for ever round the
globe; the waves the highest anywhere known.
The *Marigold* went down in the tremendous
encounter. Captain Winter, in the *Elizabeth*,
made his way back into Magellan's Straits.
There he lay for three weeks, lighting fires
nightly to show Drake where he was, but no
Drake appeared. They had agreed, if separated,
to meet on the coast in the latitude of Valparaiso;
but Winter was chicken-hearted, or else traitorous
like Doughty, and sore, we are told, 'against the
mariners' will,' when the three weeks were out,
he sailed away for England, where he reported

that all the ships were lost but the *Pelican*, and
that the *Pelican* was probably lost too.

Drake had believed better of Winter, and had
not expected to be so deserted.   He had himself
taken refuge among the islands which form the
Cape, waiting for the spring and milder weather.
He used the time in making surveys, and observ-
ing the habits of the native Patagonians, whom
he found a tough race, going naked amidst ice
and snow.   The days lengthened, and the sea
smoothed at last.   He then sailed for Valparaiso,
hoping to meet Winter there, as he had arranged.
At Valparaiso there was no Winter, but there was
in the port instead a great galleon just come in
from Peru.   The galleon's crew took him for a
Spaniard, hoisted their colours, and beat their
drums.   The *Pelican* shot alongside.   The English
sailors in high spirits leapt on board.   A Plymouth
lad who could speak Spanish knocked down the
first man he met with an 'Abajo, perro!' 'Down,
you dog, down!'   No life was taken; Drake
never hurt man if he could help it.   The crew
crossed themselves, jumped overboard, and swam
ashore.   The prize was examined.   Four hundred

pounds' weight of gold was found in her, besides
other plunder.

The galleon being disposed of, Drake and his
men pulled ashore to look at the town. The
people had all fled. In the church they found
a chalice, two cruets, and an altar-cloth, which
were made over to the chaplain to improve his
Communion furniture. A few pipes of wine and
a Greek pilot who knew the way to Lima completed the booty.

'Shocking piracy,' you will perhaps say. But
what Drake was doing would have been all right
and good service had war been declared, and the
essence of things does not alter with the form.
In essence there *was* war, deadly war, between
Philip and Elizabeth. Even later, when the
Armada sailed, there had been no formal declaration. The reality is the important part of the
matter. It was but stroke for stroke, and the
English arm proved the stronger.

Still hoping to find Winter in advance of him,
Drake went on next to Tarapaca, where silver
from the Andes mines was shipped for Panama.
At Tarapaca there was the same unconsciousness

of danger. The silver bars lay piled on the quay, the muleteers who had brought them were sleeping peacefully in the sunshine at their side. The muleteers were left to their slumbers. The bars were lifted into the English boats. A train of mules or llamas came in at the moment with a second load as rich as the first. This, too, went into the *Pelican's* hold. The bullion taken at Tarapaca was worth near half a million ducats.

Still there were no news of Winter. Drake began to realise that he was now entirely alone, and had only himself and his own crew to depend on. There was nothing to do but to go through with it, danger adding to the interest. Arica was the next point visited. Half a hundred blocks of silver were picked up at Arica. After Arica came Lima, the chief depôt of all, where the grandest haul was looked for. At Lima, alas! they were just too late. Twelve great hulks lay anchored there. The sails were unbent, the men were ashore. They contained nothing but some chests of reals and a few bales of silk and linen. But a thirteenth, called by the gods *Our Lady of the Conception*, called by men *Cacafuego*, a name

incapable of translation, had sailed a few days
before for the isthmus, with the whole produce of
the Lima mines for the season. Her ballast was
silver, her cargo gold and emeralds and rubies.

Drake deliberately cut the cables of the ships
in the roads, that they might drive ashore and be
unable to follow him. The *Pelican* spread her
wings, every feather of them, and sped away in
pursuit. He would know the *Cacafuego*, so he
learnt at Lima, by the peculiar cut of her sails.
The first man who caught sight of her was
promised a gold chain for his reward. A sail
was seen on the second day. It was not the
chase, but it was worth stopping for. Eighty
pounds' weight of gold was found, and a great
gold crucifix, set with emeralds said to be as large
as pigeon's eggs. They took the kernel. They
left the shell. Still on and on. We learn from
the Spanish accounts that the Viceroy of Lima,
as soon as he recovered from his astonishment,
despatched ships in pursuit. They came up with
the last plundered vessel, heard terrible tales of
the rovers' strength, and went back for a larger
force. The *Pelican* meanwhile went along upon

her course for 800 miles. At length, when in
the latitude of Quito and close under the shore,
the *Cacafuego's* peculiar sails were sighted, and the
gold chain was claimed. There she was, freighted
with the fruit of Aladdin's garden, going lazily
along a few miles ahead. Care was needed in
approaching her. If she guessed the *Pelican's*
character, she would run in upon the land and
they would lose her. It was afternoon. The sun
was still above the horizon, and Drake meant to
wait till night, when the breeze would be off the
shore, as in the tropics it always is.

The *Pelican* sailed two feet to the *Cacafuego's*
one. Drake filled his empty wine-skins with
water and trailed them astern to stop his way.
The chase supposed that she was followed by
some heavy-loaded trader, and, wishing for company on a lonely voyage, she slackened sail and
waited for him to come up. At length the sun
went down into the ocean, the rosy light faded
from off the snows of the Andes; and when both
ships had become invisible from the shore, the
skins were hauled in, the night wind rose, and
the water began to ripple under the *Pelican's*

bows. The *Cacafuego* was swiftly overtaken, and
when within a cable's length a voice hailed her
to put her head into the wind. The Spanish
commander, not understanding so strange an
order, held on his course. A broadside brought
down his mainyard, and a flight of arrows rattled
on his deck. He was himself wounded. In a few
minutes he was a prisoner, and *Our Lady of the
Conception* and her precious freight were in the
corsair's power. The wreck was cut away; the
ship was cleared; a prize crew was put on board.
Both vessels turned their heads to the sea. At
daybreak no land was to be seen, and the examination of the prize began.   The full value was
never acknowledged. The invoice, if there was
one, was destroyed. The accurate figures were
known only to Drake and Queen Elizabeth. A
published schedule acknowledged to twenty tons
of silver bullion, thirteen chests of silver coins,
and a hundredweight of gold, but there were gold
nuggets besides in indefinite quantity, and 'a
great store' of pearls, emeralds, and diamonds.
The Spanish Government proved a loss of a
million and a half of ducats, excluding what

belonged to private persons. The total capture was immeasurably greater.

Drake, we are told, was greatly satisfied. He thought it prudent to stay in the neighbourhood no longer than necessary. He went north with all sail set, taking his prize along with him. The master, San Juan de Anton, was removed on board the *Pelican* to have his wound attended to. He remained as Drake's guest for a week, and sent in a report of what he observed to the Spanish Government. One at least of Drake's party spoke excellent Spanish. This person took San Juan over the ship. She showed signs, San Juan said, of rough service, but was still in fine condition, with ample arms, spare rope, mattocks, carpenters' tools of all descriptions. There were eighty-five men on board all told, fifty of them men-of-war, the rest young fellows, ship-boys and the like. Drake himself was treated with great reverence; a sentinel stood always at his cabin door. He dined alone with music.

No mystery was made of the *Pelican's* exploits. The chaplain showed San Juan the crucifix set with emeralds, and asked him if he could seriously believe that to be God. San Juan asked Drake how he meant to go home. Drake showed him a globe with three courses traced on it. There was the way that he had come, there was the way by China and the Cape of Good Hope, and there was a third way which he did not explain. San Juan asked if Spain and England were at war. Drake said he had a commission from the Queen. His captures were for her, not for himself. He added afterwards that the Viceroy of Mexico had robbed him and his kinsman, and he was making good his losses.

Then, touching the point of the sore, he said, ' I know the Viceroy will send for thee to inform himself of my proceedings. Tell him he shall do well to put no more Englishmen to death, and to spare those he has in his hands, for if he do execute them I will hang 2,000 Spaniards and send him their heads.'

After a week's detention San Juan and his men were restored to the empty *Cacafuego,* and allowed to go. On their way back they fell in with the two cruisers sent in pursuit from Lima, reinforced by a third from Panama. They were

now fully armed ; they went in chase, and according to their own account came up with the *Pelican*.
But, like Lope de Vega, they seemed to have
been terrified at Drake as a sort of devil. They
confessed that they dared not attack him, and
again went back for more assistance. The Viceroy
abused them as cowards, arrested the officers,
despatched others again with peremptory orders
to seize Drake, even if he was the devil, but by
that time their questionable visitor had flown.
They found nothing, perhaps to their relief.

A despatch went instantly across the Atlantic
to Philip. One squadron was sent off from Cadiz
to watch the Straits of Magellan, and another to
patrol the Caribbean Sea. It was thought that
Drake's third way was no seaway at all, that he
meant to leave the *Pelican* at Darien, carry his
plunder over the mountains, and build a ship at
Honduras to take him home. His real idea was
that he might hit off the passage to the north of
which Frobisher and Davis thought they had
found the eastern entrance. He stood on towards
California, picking up an occasional straggler in
the China trade, with silk, porcelain, gold, and

emeralds. Fresh water was a necessity. He put
in at Guatulco for it, and his proceedings were
humorously prompt. The alcaldes at Guatulco
were in session trying a batch of negroes. An
English boat's crew appeared in court, tied the
alcaldes hand and foot, and carried them off to
the *Pelican*, there to remain as hostages till the
water-casks were filled.

North again he fell in with a galleon carrying
out a new Governor to the Philippines. The
Governor was relieved of his boxes and his jewels,
and then, says one of the party, 'Our General,
thinking himself in respect of his private injuries
received from the Spaniards, as also their contempt and indignities offered to our country and
Prince, sufficiently satisfied and revenged, and
supposing her Majesty would rest contented with
this service, began to consider the best way home.'
The first necessity was a complete overhaul of the
ship. Before the days of copper sheathing weeds
grew thick under water. Barnacles formed in
clusters, stopping the speed, and sea-worms bored
through the planking. Twenty thousand miles
lay between the *Pelican* and Plymouth Sound,

and Drake was not a man to run idle chances. Still holding his north course till he had left the furthest Spanish settlement far to the south, he put into Canoas Bay in California, laid the *Pelican* ashore, set up forge and workshop, and repaired and re-rigged her with a month's labour from stem to stern. With every rope new set up and new canvas on every yard, he started again on April 16, 1579, and continued up the coast to Oregon. The air grew cold though it was summer. The men felt it from having been so long in the tropics, and dropped out of health. There was still no sign of a passage. If passage there was, Drake perceived that it must be of enormous length. Magellan's Straits, he guessed, would be watched for him, so he decided on the route by the Cape of Good Hope. In the Philippine ship he had found a chart of the Indian Archipelago. With the help of this and his own skill he hoped to find his way. He went down again to San Francisco, landed there, found the soil teeming with gold, made acquaintance with an Indian king who hated the Spaniards and wished to become an English subject. But Drake

K

had no leisure to annex new territories. Avoiding
the course from Mexico to the Philippines, he
made a direct course to the Moluccas, and brought
up again at the Island of Celebes. Here the
Pelican was a second time docked and scraped.
The crew had a month's rest among the fireflies
and vampires of the tropical forest. Leaving
Celebes, they entered on the most perilous part
of the whole voyage. They wound their way
among coral reefs and low islands scarcely visible
above the water-line. In their chart the only
outlet marked into the Indian Ocean was by the
Straits of Malacca. But Drake guessed rightly
that there must be some nearer opening, and felt
his way looking for it along the coast of Java.
Spite of all his care, he was once on the edge
of destruction. One evening as night was closing
in a grating sound was heard under the *Pelican's*
keel. In another moment she was hard and
fast on a reef. The breeze was light and the
water smooth, or the world would have heard no
more of Francis Drake. She lay immovable
till daybreak. At dawn the position was seen
not to be entirely desperate. Drake himself

showed all the qualities of a great commander.
Cannon were thrown over and cargo that was not
needed.   In the afternoon, the wind changing, the
lightened vessel lifted off the rocks and was saved.
The hull was uninjured, thanks to the Californian
repairs.   All on board had behaved well with the
one exception of Mr. Fletcher, the chaplain.   Mr.
Fletcher, instead of working like a man, had
whined about Divine retribution for the execution of Doughty.

For the moment Drake passed it over.   A few
days after, they passed out through the Straits of
Sunda, where they met the great ocean swell,
Homer's μέγα κῦμα θαλάσσης, and they knew then
that all was well.

There was now time to call Mr. Fletcher to
account.   It was no business of the chaplain to
discourage and dispirit men in a moment of
danger, and a court was formed to sit upon him.
An English captain on his own deck represents
the sovereign, and is head of Church as well as
State.   Mr. Fletcher was brought to the forecastle,
where Drake, sitting on a sea-chest with a pair
of *pantoufles* in his hand, excommunicated him,

pronounced him cut off from the Church of God, given over to the devil for the chastising of his flesh, and left him chained by the leg to a ring-bolt to repent of his cowardice.

In the general good-humour punishment could not be of long duration. The next day the poor chaplain had his absolution, and returned to his berth and his duty. The *Pelican* met with no more adventures. Sweeping in fine clear weather round the Cape of Good Hope, she touched once for water at Sierra Leone, and finally sailed in triumph into Plymouth Harbour, where she had been long given up for lost, having traced the first furrow round the globe. Winter had come home eighteen months before, but could report nothing. The news of the doings on the American coast had reached England through Madrid. The Spanish ambassador had been furious. It was known that Spanish squadrons had been sent in search. Complications would arise if Drake brought his plunder home, and timid politicians hoped that he was at the bottom of the sea. But here he was, actually arrived with a monarch's ransom in his hold.

English sympathy with an extraordinary exploit is always irresistible. Shouts of applause rang through the country, and Elizabeth, every bit of her an Englishwoman, felt with her subjects. She sent for Drake to London, made him tell his story over and over again, and was never weary of listening to him. As to injury to Spain, Philip had lighted a fresh insurrection in Ireland, which had cost her dearly in lives and money. For Philip to demand compensation of England on the score of justice was a thing to make the gods laugh.

So thought the Queen. So unfortunately did not think some members of her Council, Lord Burghley among them. Mendoza was determined that Drake should be punished and the spoils disgorged, or else that he would force Elizabeth upon the world as the confessed protectress of piracy. Burghley thought that, as things stood, some satisfaction (or the form of it) would have to be made.

Elizabeth hated paying back as heartily as Falstaff, nor had she the least intention of throwing to the wolves a gallant Englishman, with

whose achievements the world was ringing. She
was obliged to allow the treasure to be registered
by a responsible official, and an account rendered
to Mendoza; but for all that she meant to keep
her own share of the spoils. She meant, too, that
Drake and his brave crew should not go unre-
warded. Drake himself should have ten thousand
pounds at least.

Her action was eminently characteristic of
her. On the score of real justice there was
no doubt at all how matters stood between herself and Philip, who had tried to dethrone and
kill her.

The *Pelican* lay still at Plymouth with the
bullion and jewels untouched. She directed that
it should be landed and scheduled. She trusted
the business to Edmund Tremayne, of Sydenham,
a neighbouring magistrate, on whom she could
depend. She told him not to be too inquisitive,
and she allowed Drake to go back and arrange
the cargo before the examination was made. Let
me now read you a letter from Tremayne himself
to Sir Francis Walsingham :—

'To give you some understanding how I have

proceeded with Mr. Drake: I have at no time
entered into the account to know more of the
value of the treasure than he made me acquainted
with; and to say truth I persuaded him to impart
to me no more than need, for so I saw him commanded in her Majesty's behalf that he should
reveal the certainty to no man living. I have
only taken notice of so much as he *has* revealed,
and the same I have seen to be weighed, registered, and packed. And to observe her Majesty's
commands for the ten thousand pounds, we agreed
he should take it out of the portion that was
landed secretly, and to remove the same out of
the place before my son Henry and I should
come to the weighing and registering of what was
left; and so it was done, and no creature living
by me made privy to it but himself; and myself
no privier to it than as you may perceive by this.

'I see nothing to charge Mr. Drake further
than he is inclined to charge himself, and withal
I must say he is inclined to advance the value to
be delivered to her Majesty, and seeking in general
to recompense all men that have been in the
case dealers with him. As I dare take an oath,

he will rather diminish his own portion than leave
any of them unsatisfied. And for his mariners
and followers I have seen here as eye-witness,
and have heard with my ears, such certain signs
of goodwill as I cannot yet see that any of them
will leave his company. The whole course of his
voyage hath showed him to be of great valour ;
but my hap has been to see some particulars,
and namely in this discharge of his company, as
doth assure me that he is a man of great government, and that by the rules of God and his book,
so as proceeding on such foundation his doings
cannot but prosper.'

The result of it all was that deductions were
made from the capture equivalent to the property
which Drake and Hawkins held themselves to
have been treacherously plundered of at San Juan
de Ulloa, with perhaps other liberal allowances for
the cost of recovery. An account on part of what
remained was then given to Mendoza. It was not
returned to him or to Philip, but was laid up in
the Tower till the final settlement of Philip's and
the Queen's claims on each other—the cost, for
one thing, of the rebellion in Ireland. Commis-

sioners met and argued and sat on ineffectually
till the Armada came and the discussion ended,
and the talk of restitution was over.   Meanwhile,
opinion varied about Drake's own doings as it has
varied since.   Elizabeth listened spellbound to his
adventures, sent for him to London again, and
walked with him publicly about the parks and
gardens.   She gave him a second ten thousand
pounds.   The *Pelican* was sent round to Dept-
ford; a royal banquet was held on board, Elizabeth attended and Drake was knighted.   Mendoza
clamoured for the treasure in the Tower to be
given up to him; Walsingham wished to give it
to the Prince of Orange; Leicester and his party
in the Council, who had helped to fit Drake out,
thought it ought to be divided among themselves,
and unless Mendoza lies they offered to share it
with him if he would agree to a private arrange-
ment.   Mendoza says he answered that he would
give twice as much to chastise such a bandit as
Drake.   Elizabeth thought it should be kept as
a captured pawn in the game, and so in fact it
remained after the deductions which we have
seen had been made.

Drake was lavish of his presents. He presented the Queen with a diamond cross and a
coronet set with splendid emeralds. He gave
Bromley, the Lord Chancellor, 800 dollars' worth
of silver plate, and as much more to other members
of the Council. The Queen wore her coronet on
New Year's Day; the Chancellor was content to
decorate his sideboard at the cost of the Catholic
King. Burghley and Sussex declined the splendid
temptation; they said they could accept no such
precious gifts from a man whose fortune had been
made by plunder.

Burghley lived to see better into Drake's
value. Meanwhile, what now are we, looking
back over our history, to say of these things—the
Channel privateering; the seizure of Alva's army
money; the sharp practice of Hawkins with the
Queen of Scots and King Philip; or this amazing
performance of Sir Francis Drake in a vessel no
larger than a second-rate yacht of a modern noble
lord?

Resolution, daring, professional skill, all historians allow to these men; but, like Burghley,
they regard what they did as piracy, not much

better, if at all better, than the later exploits of
Morgan and Kidd. So cried the Catholics who
wished Elizabeth's ruin; so cried Lope de Vega
and King Philip. In milder language the modern
philosopher repeats the unfavourable verdict, re-
joices that he lives in an age when such doings are
impossible, and apologises faintly for the excesses
of an imperfect age. May I remind the philosopher
that we live in an age when other things have
also happily become impossible, and that if he and
his friends were liable when they went abroad for
their summer tours to be snapped by the familiars
of the Inquisition, whipped, burnt alive, or sent to
the galleys, he would perhaps think more leniently
of any measures by which that respectable institution and its masters might be induced to treat
philosophers with greater consideration?

Again, remember Dr. Johnson's warning,
Beware of cant. In that intensely serious century
men were more occupied with the realities than
the forms of things. By encouraging rebellion in
England and Ireland, by burning so many scores
of poor English seamen and merchants in fools'
coats at Seville, the King of Spain had given

Elizabeth a hundred occasions for declaring war against him. Situated as she was, with so many disaffected Catholic subjects, she could not *begin* a war on such a quarrel. She had to use such resources as she had, and of these resources the best was a splendid race of men who were not afraid to do for her at their own risk what commissioned officers would and might have justly done had formal war been declared, men who defeated the national enemy with materials conquered from himself, who were devoted enough to dispense with the personal security which the sovereign's commission would have extended to prisoners of war, and face the certainty of being hanged if they were taken. Yes; no doubt by the letter of the law of nations Drake and Hawkins were corsairs of the same stuff as Ulysses, as the rovers of Norway. But the common-sense of Europe saw through the form to the substance which lay below it, and the instinct of their countrymen gave them a place among the fighting heroes of England, from which I do not think they will be deposed by the eventual verdict of history.

LECTURE V

PARTIES IN THE STATE

ON December 21, 1585, a remarkable scene took place in the English House of Commons. The Prince of Orange, after many attempts had failed, had been successfully disposed of in the Low Countries. A fresh conspiracy had just been discovered for a Catholic insurrection in England, supported by a foreign invasion; the object of which was to dethrone Elizabeth and to give her crown to Mary Stuart. The Duke of Alva, at the time of the Ridolfi plot, had pointed out as a desirable preliminary, if the invasion was to succeed, the assassination of the Queen of England. The succession being undecided, he had calculated that the confusion would paralyse resistance, and the notorious favour with which Mary Stuart's pretensions were regarded by a powerful English

party would ensure her an easy victory were
Elizabeth once removed. But this was an indis-
pensable condition. It had become clear at last
that so long as Elizabeth was alive Philip would
not willingly sanction the landing of a Spanish
army on English shores. Thus, among the more
ardent Catholics, especially the refugees at the
Seminary at Rheims, a crown in heaven was held
out to any spiritual knight-errant who would
remove the obstacle. The enterprise itself was
not a difficult one. Elizabeth was aware of her
danger, but she was personally fearless. She
refused to distrust the Catholics. Her household
was full of them. She admitted anyone to her
presence who desired a private interview. Dr.
Parry, a member of Parliament, primed by en-
couragements from the Cardinal of Como and the
Vatican, had undertaken to risk his life to win
the glorious prize. He introduced himself into
the palace, properly provided with arms. He
professed to have information of importance to
give. The Queen received him repeatedly. Once
he was alone with her in the palace garden,
and was on the point of killing her, when he was

awed, as he said, by the likeness to her father. Parry was discovered and hanged, but Elizabeth refused to take warning. When there were so many aspirants for the honour of removing Jezebel, and Jezebel was so easy of approach, it was felt that one would at last succeed; and the loyal part of the nation, led by Lord Burghley, formed themselves into an association to protect a life so vital to them and apparently so indifferent to herself.

The subscribers bound themselves to pursue to the death all manner of persons who should attempt or consent to anything to the harm of her Majesty's person; never to allow or submit to any pretended successor by whom or for whom such detestable act should be attempted or committed; but to pursue such persons to death and act the utmost revenge upon them.

The bond in its first form was a visible creation of despair. It implied a condition of things in which order would have ceased to exist. The lawyers, who, it is curious to observe, were generally in Mary Stuart's interest, vehemently objected; yet so passionate was public feeling that it was signed throughout the kingdom, and Parliament was called to pass an Act which would secure the same object. Mary Stuart, at any rate, was not to benefit by the crimes either of herself or her admirers. It was provided that if the realm was invaded, or a rebellion instigated by or for any one pretending a title to the crown after the Queen's death, such pretender should be disqualified for ever. In the event of the Queen's assassination the government was to devolve on a Committee of Peers and Privy Councillors, who were to examine the particulars of the murder and execute the perpetrators and their accomplices; while, with a significant allusion, all Jesuits and seminary priests were required to leave the country instantly, under pain of death.

The House of Commons was heaving with emotion when the Act was sent up to the Peers. To give expression to their burning feelings Sir Christopher Hatton proposed that before they separated they should join him in a prayer for the Queen's preservation. The 400 members all rose, and knelt on the floor of the House, repeating Hatton's words after him, sentence by sentence.

Jesuits and seminary priests! Attempts have been made to justify the conspiracies against Elizabeth from what is called the persecution of the innocent enthusiasts who came from Rheims to preach the Catholic faith to the English people. Popular writers and speakers dwell on the executions of Campian and his friends as worse than the Smithfield burnings, and amidst general admiration and approval these martyred saints have been lately canonised. Their mission, it is said, was purely religious. Was it so? The chief article in the religion which they came to teach was the duty of obedience to the Pope, who had excommunicated the Queen, had absolved her subjects from their allegiance, and, by a relaxation of the Bull, had permitted them to pretend to loyalty *ad illud tempus*, till a Catholic army of deliverance should arrive. A Pope had sent a legate to Ireland, and was at that moment stirring up a bloody insurrection there.

But what these seminary priests were, and what their object was, will best appear from an account of the condition of England, drawn up for the use of the Pope and Philip, by Father

L

Parsons, who was himself at the head of the
mission. The date of it is 1585, almost simul-
taneous with the scene in Parliament which I
have just been describing. The English refugees,
from Cardinal Pole downwards, were the most
active and passionate preachers of a Catholic
crusade against England. They failed, but they
have revenged themselves in history. Pole,
Sanders, Allen,. and Parsons have coloured all
that we suppose ourselves to know of Henry VIII.
and Elizabeth. What I am about to read to you
does not differ essentially from what we have
already heard from these persons; but it is new,
and, being intended for practical guidance, is
complete in its way. It comes from the Spanish
archives, and is not therefore open to suspicion.
Parsons, as you know, was a Fellow of Balliol
before his conversion; Allen was a Fellow of Oriel,
and Sanders of New College. An Oxford Church
of England education is an excellent thing, and
beautiful characters have been formed in the
Catholic universities abroad; but as the elements
of dynamite are innocent in themselves, yet when
fused together produce effects no one would have

dreamt of, so Oxford and Rome, when they have
run together, have always generated a somewhat
furious compound.

Parsons describes his statement as a ' brief note
on the present condition of England,' from which
may be inferred the ease and opportuneness of
the holy enterprise. ' England,' he says, ' contains
fifty-two counties, of which forty are well inclined
to the Catholic faith. Heretics in these are few,
and are hated by all ranks. The remaining twelve
are infected more or less, but even in these the
Catholics are in the majority. Divide England
into three parts; two-thirds at least are Catholic
at heart, though many conceal their convictions
in fear of the Queen. English Catholics are of
two sorts—one which makes an open profession
regardless of consequences, the other believing at
the bottom, but unwilling to risk life or fortune,
and so submitting outwardly to the heretic laws,
but as eager as the Catholic confessors for
redemption from slavery.

' The Queen and her party,' he goes on, ' more
fear these secret Catholics than those who wear
their colours openly. The latter they can fine,

disarm, and make innocuous. The others, being outwardly compliant, cannot be touched, nor can any precaution be taken against their rising when the day of divine vengeance shall arrive.

'The counties specially Catholic are the most warlike, and contain harbours and other conveniences for the landing of an invading army. The north towards the Scotch border has been trained in constant fighting. The Scotch nobles on the other side are Catholic and will lend their help. So will all Wales.

'The inhabitants of the midland and southern provinces, where the taint is deepest, are indolent and cowardly, and do not know what war means. The towns are more corrupt than the country districts. But the strength of England does not lie, as on the Continent, in towns and cities. The town population are merchants and craftsmen, rarely or never nobles or magnates.

'The nobility, who have the real power, reside with their retinues in castles scattered over the land. The wealthy yeomen are strong and honest, all attached to the ancient faith, and may be counted on when an attempt is made for the restoration of it. The knights and gentry are generally well affected also, and will be well to the front. Many of their sons are being now educated in our seminaries. Some are in exile, but all, whether at home or abroad, will be active on our side.

'Of the great peers, marquises, earls, viscounts, and barons, part are with us, part against us. But the latter sort are new creations, whom the Queen has promoted either for heresy or as her personal lovers, and therefore universally abhorred.

'The premier peer of the old stock is the Earl of Arundel, son and heir of the late Duke of Norfolk, whom she has imprisoned because he tried to escape out of the realm. This earl is entirely Catholic, as well as his brothers and kinsmen; and they have powerful vassals who are eager to revenge the injury of their lord. The Earl of Northumberland and his brothers are Catholics. They too have family wrongs to repay, their father having been this year murdered in the Tower, and they have placed themselves at my disposal. The Earl of Worcester and his heir hate heresy, and are devoted to us with all their dependents. The Earls of Cumberland and Southampton and Viscount Montague are faithful, and have a large following. Besides these we have many of the barons—Dacre, Morley, Vaux, Windsor, Wharton, Lovelace, Stourton, and others besides. The Earl of Westmoreland, with Lord Paget and Sir Francis Englefield, who reside abroad, have been incredibly earnest in promoting our enterprise. With such support, it is impossible that we can fail. These lords and gentlemen, when they see efficient help coming to them, will certainly rise, and for the following reasons :—

' 1. Because some of the principals among them have given me their promise.

' 2. Because, on hearing that Pope Pius intended to excommunicate and depose the Queen sixteen years ago, many Catholics did rise. They only failed because no support was sent them, and the Pope's sentence had not at that time been actually published. Now, when the Pope has spoken and help is certain, there is not a doubt how they will act.

' 3. Because the Catholics are now much more

numerous, and have received daily instruction in their religion from our priests. There is now no orthodox Catholic in the whole realm who supposes that he is any longer bound in conscience to obey the Queen. Books for the occasion have been written and published by us, in which we prove that it is not only lawful for Catholics, but their positive duty, to fight against the Queen and heresy when the Pope bids them; and these books are so greedily read among them that when the time comes they are certain to take arms.

'4. The Catholics in these late years have shown their real feeling in the martyrdoms of priests and laymen, and in attempts made by several of them against the person and State of the Queen. Various Catholics have tried to kill her at the risk of their own lives, and are still trying.

'5. We have three hundred priests dispersed among the houses of the nobles and honest gentry. Every day we add to their number; and these priests will direct the consciences and actions of the Catholics at the great crisis.

'6. They have been so harried and so worried

that they hate the heretics worse than they hate
the Turks.

'Should any of them fear the introduction of
a Spanish army as dangerous to their national
liberties, there is an easy way to satisfy their
scruples. Let it be openly declared that the
enterprise is undertaken in the name of the Pope,
and there will be no more hesitation. We have
ourselves prepared a book for their instruction, to
be issued at the right moment. If his Holiness
desires to see it we will have it translated into
Latin for his use.

'Before the enterprise is undertaken the
sentence of excommunication and deposition ought
to be reissued, with special clauses.

'It must be published in all adjoining Catholic
countries; all Catholic kings and princes must be
admonished to forbid every description of inter-
course with the pretended Queen and her heretic
subjects, and themselves especially to make or
observe no treaties with her, to send no embassies
to her and admit none; to render no help to her
of any sort or kind.

'Besides those who will be our friends for re-

ligion's sake we shall have others with us—neutrals
or heretics of milder sort, or atheists, with whom
England now abounds, who will join us in the
interest of the Queen of Scots.   Among them are
the Marquis of Winchester, the Earls of Shrewsbury, Derby, Oxford, Rutland, and several other
peers.   The Queen of Scots herself will be of
infinite assistance to us in securing these.   She
knows who are her secret friends.   She has been
able so far, and we trust will always be able, to
communicate with them.   She will see that they
are ready at the right time.   She has often written
to me to say that she hopes that she will be able
to escape when the time comes.   In her last letter
she urges me to be vehement with his Holiness
in pushing on the enterprise, and bids him have no
concern for her own safety.   She believes that she
can care for herself.   If not, she says she will lose
her life willingly in a cause so sacred.

'The enemies that we shall have to deal with
are the more determined heretics whom we call
Puritans, and certain creatures of the Queen, the
Earls of Leicester and Huntingdon, and a few
others.   They will have an advantage in the money

in the Treasury, the public arms and stores, and the army and navy, but none of them have ever seen a camp. The leaders have been nuzzled in love-making and Court pleasures, and they will all fly at the first shock of war. They have not a man who can command in the field. In the whole realm there are but two fortresses which could stand a three days' siege. The people are enervated by long peace, and, except a few who have served with the heretics in Flanders, cannot bear their arms. Of those few some are dead and some have deserted to the Prince of Parma, a clear proof of the real disposition to revolt. There is abundance of food and cattle in the country, all of which will be at our service and cannot be kept from us. Everywhere there are safe and roomy harbours, almost all undefended. An invading force can be landed with ease, and there will be no lack of local pilots. Fifteen thousand trained soldiers will be sufficient, aided by the Catholic English, though, of course, the larger the force, particularly if it includes cavalry, the quicker the work will be done and the less the expense. Practically there will be nothing to overcome save an unwarlike and undisciplined mob.

'Sixteen times England has been invaded. Twice only the native race have repelled the attacking force. They have been defeated on every other occasion, and with a cause so holy and just as ours we need not fear to fail. The expenses shall be repaid to his Holiness and the Catholic King out of the property of the heretics and the Protestant clergy. There will be ample in these resources to compensate all who give us their hand. But the work must be done promptly. Delay will be infinitely dangerous. If we put off, as we have done hitherto, the Catholics will be tired out and reduced in numbers and strength. The nobles and priests now in exile, and able to be of such service, will break down in poverty. The Queen of Scots may be executed or die a natural death, or something may happen to the Catholic King or his Holiness. The Queen of England may herself die, a heretic Government may be reconstructed under a heretic successor, the young Scotch king or some other, and our case will then be desperate; whereas if we can prevent this and save the Queen of Scots there will be good hope of converting her son and reducing the whole island to the obedience of the faith. Now is the moment. The French Government cannot interfere. The Duke of Guise will help us for the sake of the faith and for his kinswoman. The Turks are quiet. The Church was never stronger or more united. Part of Italy is under the Catholic King; the rest is in league with his Holiness. The revolt in the Low Countries is all but crushed. The sea provinces are on the point of surrendering. If they give up the contest their harbours will be at our service for the invasion. If not, the way to conquer them is to conquer England.

'I need not urge how much it imports his Holiness to undertake this glorious work. He, supremely wise as he is, knows that from this Jezebel and her supporters come all the perils which disturb the Christian world. He knows that heretical depravity and all other miseries can only end when this woman is chastised. Reverence for his Holiness and love for my afflicted country force me to speak. I submit to his most holy judgment myself and my advice.'

The most ardent Catholic apologist will hardly
maintain, in the face of this document, that the
English Jesuits and seminary priests were the
innocent missionaries of religion which the modern
enemies of Elizabeth's Government describe them.
Father Parsons, the writer of it, was himself the
leader and director of the Jesuit invasion, and
cannot be supposed to have misrepresented the
purpose for which they had been sent over. The
point of special interest is the account which he
gives of the state of parties and general feeling in
the English people. Was there that wide disposition to welcome an invading army in so large a
majority of the nation? The question is supposed
to have been triumphantly answered three years
later, when it is asserted that the difference of
creed was forgotten, and Catholics and Protestants
fought side by side for the liberties of England.
But, in the first place, the circumstances were
changed. The Queen of Scots no longer lived,
and the success of the Armada implied a foreign
sovereign. But, next, the experiment was not
tried. The battle was fought at sea, by a fleet
four-fifths of which was composed of Protestant

adventurers, fitted out and manned by those zeal-
ous Puritans whose fidelity to the Queen Parsons
himself admitted. Lord Howard may have been
an Anglo-Catholic; Roman Catholic he never
was; but he and his brother were the only loyalists
in the House of Howard. Arundel and the rest
of his kindred were all that Parsons claimed for
them. How the country levies would have behaved had Parma landed is still uncertain. It is
likely that if the Spanish army had gained a first
success, there might have been some who would
have behaved as Sir William Stanley did. It is
observable that Parsons mentions Leicester and
Huntingdon as the only powerful peers on whom
the Queen could rely, and Leicester, otherwise the
unfittest man in her dominions, she chose to
command her land army.

The Duke of Alva and his master Philip, both
of them distrusted political priests. Political
priests, they said, did not understand the facts
of things. Theological enthusiasm made them
credulous of what they wished. But Father
Parsons's estimate is confirmed in all its parts by
the letters of Mendoza, the Spanish ambassador

in London. Mendoza was himself a soldier, and
his first duty was to learn the real truth. It may
be taken as certain that, with the Queen of Scots
still alive to succeed to the throne, at the time of
the scene in the House of Commons, with which
I began this lecture, the great majority of the
country party disliked the Reformers, and were
looking forward to the accession of a Catholic
sovereign, and as a consequence to a religious
revolution.

It explains the difficulty of Elizabeth's position and the inconsistency of her political action.
Burghley, Walsingham, Mildmay, Knolles, the
elder Bacon, were believing Protestants, and
would have had her put herself openly at the
head of a Protestant European league. They
believed that right and justice were on their side,
that their side was God's cause, as they called it,
and that God would care for it. Elizabeth had
no such complete conviction. She disliked dog-
matism, Protestant as well as Catholic. She
ridiculed Mr. Cecil and his brothers in Christ.
She thought, like Erasmus, that the articles of
faith, for which men were so eager to kill one

another, were subjects which they knew very
little about, and that every man might think
what he would on such matters without injury to
the commonwealth. To become 'head of the
name' would involve open war with the Catholic
powers. War meant war taxes, which more than
half her subjects would resent or resist. Religion
as she understood it was a development of law—
the law of moral conduct. You could not have
two laws in one country, and you could not have
two religions; but the outward form mattered
comparatively little. The people she ruled over
were divided about these forms. They were
mainly fools, and if she let them each have
chapels and churches of their own, molehills would
become mountains, and the congregations would
go from arguing into fighting. With Parliament
to help her, therefore, she established a Liturgy,
in which those who wished to find the Mass could
hear the Mass, while those who wanted predestin-
ation and justification by faith could find it in the
Articles. Both could meet under a common roof,
and use a common service, if they would only be
reasonable. If they would not be reasonable, the

Catholics might have their own ritual in their own houses, and would not be interfered with.

This system continued for the first eleven years of Elizabeth's reign. No Catholic, she could proudly say, had ever during that time been molested for his belief. There was a small fine for non-attendance at church, but even this was rarely levied, and by the confession of the Jesuits the Queen's policy was succeeding too well. Sensible men began to see that the differences of religion were not things to quarrel over. Faith was growing languid. The elder generation, who had lived through the Edward and Mary revolutions, were satisfied to be left undisturbed; a new generation was growing up, with new ideas; and so the Church of Rome bestirred itself. Elizabeth was excommunicated. The cycle began of intrigue and conspiracy, assassination plots, and Jesuit invasions. Punishments had to follow, and in spite of herself Elizabeth was driven into what the Catholics could call religious persecution. Religious it was not, for the seminary priests were missionaries of treason. But religious it was made to appear. The English gentleman who wished to remain loyal, without forfeiting his faith, was taught to see that a sovereign under the Papal curse had no longer a claim on his allegiance. If he disobeyed the Pope, he had ceased to be a member of the Church of Christ. The Papal party grew in coherence, while, opposed to them as their purpose came in view, the Protestants, who at first had been inclined to Lutheranism, adopted the deeper and sterner creed of Calvin and Geneva. The memories of the Marian cruelties revived again. They saw themselves threatened with a return to stake and fagot. They closed their ranks and resolved to die rather than submit again to Antichrist. They might be inferior in numbers. A *plébiscite* in England at that moment would have sent Burghley and Walsingham to the scaffold. But the Lord could save by few as well as by many. Judah had but two tribes out of the twelve, but the words of the men of Judah were fiercer than the words of Israel.

One great mistake had been made by Parsons. He could not estimate what he could not understand. He admitted that the inhabitants of the

towns were mainly heretic — London, Bristol,
Plymouth, and the rest—but he despised them as
merchants, craftsmen, mean persons who had no
heart to fight in them. Nothing is more remarkable in the history of the sixteenth century than
the effect of Calvinism in levelling distinctions of
rank and in steeling and ennobling the character
of common men. In Scotland, in the Low
Countries, in France, there was the same phenomenon. In Scotland, the Kirk was the creation
of the preachers and the people, and peasants and
workmen dared to stand in the field against belted
knights and barons, who had trampled on their
fathers for centuries. The artisans of the Low
Countries had for twenty years defied the whole
power of Spain. The Huguenots were not a fifth
part of the French nation, yet defeat could never
dishearten them. Again and again they forced
Crown and nobles to make terms with them.
It was the same in England. The allegiance
to their feudal leaders dissolved into a higher
obligation to the King of kings, whose elect they
believed themselves to be. Election to them was
not a theological phantasm, but an enlistment in

the army of God. A little flock they might be,
but they were a dangerous people to deal with,
most of all in the towns on the sea. The sea was
the element of the Reformers. The Popes had
no jurisdiction over the winds and waves. Rochelle
was the citadel of the Huguenots. The English
merchants and mariners had wrongs of their own,
perpetually renewed, which fed the bitterness of
their indignation. Touch where they would in
Spanish ports, the inquisitor's hand was on their
ships' crews, and the crews, unless they denied
their faith, were handed over to the stake or the
galleys. The Calvinists are accused of intolerance.
I fancy that even in these humane and enlightened
days we should not be very tolerant if the King
of Dahomey were to burn every European visitor
to his dominions who would not worship Mumbo
Jumbo. The Duke of Alva was not very merciful
to heretics, but he tried to bridle the zeal of the
Holy Office in burning the English seamen.
Even Philip himself remonstrated. It was to no
purpose. The Holy Office said they would think
about it, but concluded to go on. I am not
the least surprised if the English seamen were

intolerant. I should be very much surprised if
they had not been. The Queen could not protect
them. They had to protect themselves as they
could, and make Spanish vessels, when they could
catch them, pay for the iniquities of their rulers.

With such a temper rising on both sides,
Elizabeth's policy had but a poor chance. She
still hoped that the better sense of mankind
would keep the doctrinal enthusiasts in order.
Elizabeth wished her subjects would be content
to live together in unity of spirit, if not in unity
of theory, in the bond of peace, not hatred, in
righteousness of life, not in orthodoxy preached
by stake and gibbet. She was content to wait
and to persevere. She refused to declare war.
War would tear the world in pieces. She knew
her danger. She knew that she was in constant
peril of assassination. She knew that if the
Protestants were crushed in Scotland, in France,
and in the Low Countries, her own turn would
follow. To protect insurgents avowedly would be
to justify insurrection against herself. But what
she would not do openly she would do secretly.
What she would not do herself she let her subjects

do. Thousands of English volunteers fought in Flanders for the States, and in France for the Huguenots. When the English Treasury was shut to the entreaties of Coligny or William of Orange the London citizens untied their purse-strings. Her friends in Scotland fared ill. They were encouraged by promises which were not observed, because to observe them might bring on war. They committed themselves for her sake. They fell one after another — Murray, Morton, Gowrie — into bloody graves. Others took their places and struggled on. The Scotch Reformation was saved. Scotland was not allowed to open its arms to an invading army to strike England across the Border. But this was held to be their sufficient recompense. They cared for their cause as well as for the English Queen, and they had their reward. If they saved her they saved their own country. She too did not lie on a bed of roses. To prevent open war she was exposing her own life to the assassin. At any moment a pistol-shot or a stab with a dagger might add Elizabeth to the list of victims. She knew it, yet she went on upon her own policy,

and faced in her person her own share of the risk.
One thing only she did. If she would not defend
her friends and her subjects as Queen of England,
she left them free to defend themselves. She
allowed traitors to be hanged when they were
caught at their work. She allowed the merchants
to fit out their privateer fleets, to defend at their
own cost the shores of England, and to teach the
Spaniards to fear their vengeance.

But how long was all this to last? How long
were loyal citizens to feel that they were living
over a loaded mine?—throughout their own
country, throughout the Continent, at Rome and
at Madrid, at Brussels and at Paris, a legion of
conspirators were driving their shafts under the
English commonwealth. The Queen might be
indifferent to her own danger, but on the Queen's
life hung the peace of the whole realm. A stroke
of a poniard, a touch of a trigger, and swords
would be flying from their scabbards in every
county; England would become, like France, one
wild scene of anarchy and civil war. No successor had been named. The Queen refused to
hear a successor declared. Mary Stuart's hand

had been in every plot since she crossed the
Border. Twice the House of Commons had
petitioned for her execution. Elizabeth would
neither touch her life nor allow her hopes of the
crown to be taken from her. The Bond of Association was but a remedy of despair, and the Act
of Parliament would have passed for little in the
tempest which would immediately rise. The
agony reached a height when the fatal news came
from the Netherlands that there at last assassination had done its work. The Prince of Orange,
after many failures, had been finished, and a libel
was found in the Palace at Westminster exhorting
the ladies of the household to provide a Judith
among themselves to rid the world of the English
Holofernes.

One part of Elizabeth's subjects, at any rate,
were not disposed to sit down in patience under
the eternal nightmare. From Spain was to come
the army of deliverance for which the Jesuits
were so passionately longing. To the Spaniards
the Pope was looking for the execution of the
Bull of Deposition. Father Parsons had left out
of his estimate the Protestant adventurers of

London and Plymouth, who, besides their creed
and their patriotism, had their private wrongs to
revenge. Philip might talk of peace, and perhaps
in weariness might at times seriously wish for it;
but between the Englishmen whose life was on
the ocean and the Spanish Inquisition, which
had burned so many of them, there was no peace
possible. To them, Spain was the natural enemy.
Among the daring spirits who had sailed with
Drake round the globe, who had waylaid the
Spanish gold ships, and startled the world with
their exploits, the joy of whose lives had been to
fight Spaniards wherever they could meet with
them, there was but one wish—for an honest
open war. The great galleons were to them no
objects of terror. The Spanish naval power
seemed to them a 'Colossus stuffed with clouts.'
They were Protestants all of them, but their
theology was rather practical than speculative.
If Italians and Spaniards chose to believe in
the Mass, it was not any affair of theirs. Their
quarrel was with the insolent pretence of Catholics to force their creed on others with sword and
cannon. The spirit which was working in them

was the genius of freedom. On their own element they felt that they could be the spiritual tyrants' masters. But as things were going, rebellion was likely to break out at home; their homesteads might be burning, their country overrun with the Prince of Parma's army, the Inquisition at their own doors, and a Catholic sovereign bringing back the fagots of Smithfield.

The Reformation at its origin was no introduction of novel heresies. It was a revolt of the laity of Europe against the profligacy and avarice of the clergy. The popes and cardinals pretended to be the representatives of Heaven. When called to account for abuse of their powers, they had behaved precisely as mere corrupt human kings and aristocracies behave. They had intrigued; they had excommunicated; they had set nation against nation, sovereigns against their subjects; they had encouraged assassination; they had made themselves infamous by horrid massacres, and had taught one half of foolish Christendom to hate the other. The hearts of the poor English seamen whose comrades had been burnt at Seville to make a Spanish holiday, thrilled

with a sacred determination to end such scenes.
The purpose that was in them broke into a wild
war-music, as the wind harp swells and screams
under the breath of the storm. I found in the
Record Office an unsigned letter of some inspired
old sea-dog, written in a bold round hand and addressed to Elizabeth. The ships' companies which
in summer served in Philip's men-of-war went in
winter in thousands to catch cod on the Banks of
Newfoundland. 'Give me five vessels,' the writer
said, 'and I will go out and sink them all, and the
galleons shall rot in Cadiz Harbour for want of
hands to sail them. But decide, Madam, and decide
quickly. Time flies, and will not return. *The wings
of man's life are plumed with the feathers of death.*'

The Queen did not decide. The five ships
were not sent, and the poor Castilian sailors
caught their cod in peace. But in spite of
herself Elizabeth was driven forward by the
tendencies of things. The death of the Prince of
Orange left the States without a Government.
The Prince of Parma was pressing them hard.
Without a leader they were lost. They offered
themselves to Elizabeth, to be incorporated in the

English Empire. They said that if she refused they must either submit to Spain or become provinces of France. The Netherlands, whether Spanish or French, would be equally dangerous to England. The Netherlands once brought back under the Pope, England's turn would come next; while to accept the proposal meant instant and desperate war, both with France and Spain too—for France would never allow England again to gain a foot on the Continent. Elizabeth knew not what to do. She would and she would not. She did not accept; she did not refuse. It was neither No nor Yes. Philip, who was as fond of indirect ways as herself, proposed to quicken her irresolution.

The harvest had failed in Galicia, and the population were starving. England grew more corn than she wanted, and, under a special promise that the crews should not be molested, a fleet of corn-traders had gone with cargoes of grain to Coruña, Bilbao, and Santander. The King of Spain, on hearing that Elizabeth was treating with the States, issued a sudden order to seize the vessels, confiscate the cargoes, and imprison the men. The order was executed.

One English ship only was lucky enough to escape by the adroitness of her commander. The *Primrose*, of London, lay in Bilbao Roads with a captain and fifteen hands. The mayor, on receiving the order, came on board to look over the ship. He then went on shore for a sufficient force to carry out the seizure. After he was gone the captain heard of the fate which was intended for him. The mayor returned with two boatloads of soldiers, stepped up the ladder, touched the captain on the shoulder, and told him he was a prisoner. The Englishmen snatched pike and cutlass, pistol and battleaxe, killed seven or eight of the Spanish boarders, threw the rest overboard, and flung stones on them as they scrambled into their boats. The mayor, who had fallen into the sea, caught a rope and was hauled up when the fight was over. The cable was cut, the sails hoisted, and in a few minutes the *Primrose* was under way for England, with the mayor of Bilbao below the hatches. No second vessel got away. If Philip had meant to frighten Elizabeth he could not have taken a worse means of doing it, for he had exasperated that particular part of the

English population which was least afraid of him. He had broken faith besides, and had seized some hundreds of merchants and sailors who had gone merely to relieve Spanish distress. Elizabeth, as usual, would not act herself. She sent no ships from her own navy to demand reparation; but she gave the adventurers a free hand. The London and Plymouth citizens determined to read Spain a lesson which should make an impression. They had the worst fears for the fate of the prisoners; but if they could not save, they could avenge them. Sir Francis Drake, who wished for nothing better than to be at work again, volunteered his services, and a fleet was collected at Plymouth of twenty-five sail, every one of them fitted out by private enterprise. No finer armament, certainly no better-equipped armament, ever left the English shores. The expenses were, of course, enormous. Of seamen and soldiers there were between two and three thousand. Drake's name was worth an army. The cost was to be recovered out of the expedition somehow; the Spaniards were to be made to pay for it; but how or when was left to Drake's judgment. This time there was no second in command sent by the friends of Spain to hang upon his arm. By universal consent he had the absolute command. His instructions were merely to inquire at Spanish ports into the meaning of the arrest. Beyond that he was left to go where he pleased and do what he pleased on his own responsibility. The Queen said frankly that if it proved convenient she intended to disown him. Drake had no objection to being disowned, so he could teach the Spaniards to be more careful how they handled Englishmen. What came of it will be the subject of the next lecture. Father Parsons said the Protestant traders of England had grown effeminate and dared not fight. In the ashes of their own smoking cities the Spaniards had to learn that Father Parsons had misread his countrymen. If Drake had been given to heroics he might have left Virgil's lines inscribed above the broken arms of Castile at St. Domingo:

En ego victa situ quam veri effeta senectus
Arma inter regum falsa formidine ludit :
Respice ad hæc.

LECTURE VI

THE GREAT EXPEDITION TO THE WEST INDIES

QUEEN ELIZABETH and her brother-in-law
of Spain were reluctant champions of oppos-
ing principles. In themselves they had no wish
to quarrel, but each was driven forward by fate
and circumstance—Philip by the genius of the
Catholic religion, Elizabeth by the enthusiasts
for freedom and by the advice of statesmen who
saw no safety for her except in daring. Both
wished for peace, and refused to see that peace
was impossible; but both were compelled to
yield to their subjects' eagerness. Philip had to
threaten England with invasion; Elizabeth had
to show Philip that England had a long arm,
which Spanish wisdom would do well to fear. It
was a singular position. Philip had outraged
orthodoxy and dared the anger of Rome by

maintaining an ambassador at Elizabeth's Court after her excommunication. He had laboured for a reconciliation with a sincerity which his secret letters make it impossible to doubt. He had condescended even to sue for it, in spite of Drake and the voyage of the *Pelican*; yet he had helped the Pope to set Ireland in a flame. He had encouraged Elizabeth's Catholic subjects in conspiracy after conspiracy. He had approved of attempts to dispose of her as he had disposed of the Prince of Orange. Elizabeth had retaliated, though with half a heart, by letting her soldiers volunteer into the service of the revolted Netherlands, by permitting English privateers to plunder the Spanish colonies, seize the gold ships, and revenge their own wrongs. Each, perhaps, had wished to show the other what an open war would cost them both, and each drew back when war appeared inevitable.

Events went their way. Holland and Zeeland, driven to extremity, had petitioned for incorporation with England; as a counter-stroke and a warning, Philip had arrested the English corn ships and imprisoned the owners and the crews.

N

Her own fleet was nothing. The safety of the
English shores depended on the spirit of the
adventurers, and she could not afford to check
the anger with which the news was received. To
accept the offer of the States was war, and war
she would not have. Herself, she would not act
at all; but in her usual way she might let her
subjects act for themselves, and plead, as Philip
pleaded in excuse for the Inquisition, that she
could not restrain them. And thus it was that
in September 1585, Sir Francis Drake found
himself with a fleet of twenty-five privateers and
2,500 men who had volunteered to serve with
him under his own command. He had no distinct
commission. The expedition had been fitted out
as a private undertaking. Neither officers nor
crews had been engaged for the service of the
Crown. They received no wages. In the eye of
the law they were pirates. They were going on
their own account to read the King of Spain a
necessary lesson and pay their expenses at the
King of Spain's cost. Young Protestant England
had taken fire. The name of Drake set every
Protestant heart burning, and hundreds of gallant

gentlemen had pressed in to join. A grandson
of Burghley had come, and Edward Winter the
Admiral's son, and Francis Knolles the Queen's
cousin, and Martin Frobisher, and Christopher
Carlile. Philip Sidney had wished to make one
also in the glory; but Philip Sidney was needed
elsewhere. The Queen's consent had been won
from her at a bold interval in her shifting moods.
The hot fit might pass away, and Burghley sent
Drake a hint to be off before her humour changed.
No word was said. On the morning of the 14th
of September the signal flag was flying from
Drake's maintop to up anchor and away. Drake,
as he admitted after, 'was not the most assured
of her Majesty's perseverance to let them go
forward.' Past Ushant he would be beyond reach
of recall. With light winds and calms they
drifted across the Bay. They fell in with a few
Frenchmen homeward-bound from the Banks, and
let them pass uninjured. A large Spanish ship
which they met next day, loaded with excellent
fresh salt fish, was counted lawful prize. The fish
was new and good, and was distributed through
the fleet. Standing leisurely on, they cleared

Finisterre and came up with the Isles of Bayona,
at the mouth of Vigo Harbour. They dropped
anchor there, and 'it was a great matter and a
royal sight to see them.' The Spanish Governor,
Don Pedro Bemadero, sent off with some astonishment to know who and what they were.
Drake answered with a question whether England
and Spain were at war, and if not why the
English merchants had been arrested. Don Pedro
could but say that he knew of no war, and for
the merchants an order had come for their release.
For reply Drake landed part of his force on the
islands, and Don Pedro, not knowing what to
make of such visitors, found it best to propitiate
them with cartloads of wine and fruit. The
weather, which had been hitherto fine, showed
signs of change. The wind rose, and the sea
with it. The anchorage was exposed, and Drake
sent Christopher Carlile, with one of his ships
and a few pinnaces, up the harbour to look out
for better shelter. Their appearance created a
panic in the town. The alarmed inhabitants
took to their boats, carrying off their property
and their Church plate. Carlile, who had a

Calvinistic objection to idolatry, took the liberty
of detaining part of these treasures. From one
boat he took a massive silver cross belonging to
the High Church at Vigo; from another an image
of Our Lady, which the sailors relieved of her
clothes and were said, when she was stripped,
to have treated with some indignity. Carlile's
report being satisfactory, the whole fleet was
brought the next day up the harbour and moored
above the town. The news had by this time
spread into the country. The Governor of Galicia
came down with all the force which he could
collect in a hurry. Perhaps he was in time to
save Vigo itself. Perhaps Drake, having other
aims in view, did not care to be detained over a
smaller object. The Governor, at any rate, saw
that the English were too strong for him to
meddle with. The best that he could look for
was to persuade them to go away on the easiest
terms. Drake and he met in boats for a parley.
Drake wanted water and fresh provisions. Drake
was to be allowed to furnish himself undisturbed.
He had secured what he most wanted. He had
shown the King of Spain that he was not in-

vulnerable in his own home dominion, and he
sailed away unmolested. Madrid was in consternation. That the English could dare insult
the first prince in Europe on the sacred soil of
the Peninsula itself seemed like a dream. The
Council of State sat for three days considering
the meaning of it. Drake's name was already
familiar in Spanish ears. It was not conceivable
that he had come only to inquire after the
arrested ships and seamen. But what could the
English Queen be about? Did she not know
that she existed only by the forbearance of
Philip? Did she know the King of Spain's
force? Did not she and her people quake?
Little England, it was said by some of these
councillors, was to be swallowed at a mouthful
by the King of half the world. The old Admiral
Santa Cruz was less confident about the swallow-
ing. He observed that England had many teeth,
and that instead of boasting of Spanish greatness
it would be better to provide against what she
might do with them. Till now the corsairs had
appeared only in twos and threes. With such
a fleet behind him Drake might go where he

pleased. He might be going to the South Seas
again. He might take Madeira if he liked, or
the Canary Islands. Santa Cruz himself thought
he would make for the West Indies and Panama,
and advised the sending out there instantly every
available ship that they had.

The gold fleet was Drake's real object. He
had information that it would be on its way to
Spain by the Cape de Verde Islands, and he had
learnt the time when it was to be expected. From
Vigo he sailed for the Canaries, looked in at
Palma, with ' intention to have taken our pleasure
there,' but found the landing dangerous and the
town itself not worth the risk. He ran on to the
Cape de Verde Islands. He had measured his
time too narrowly. The gold fleet had arrived
and had gone. He had missed it by twelve hours,
' the reason,' as he said with a sigh, ' best known
to God.' The chance of prize-money was lost,
but the political purpose of the expedition could
still be completed. The Cape de Verde Islands
could not sail away, and a beginning could be
made with Sant Iago. Sant Iago was a thriving,
well-populated town, and down in Drake's book

as specially needing notice, some Plymouth sailors
haing been recently murdered there. Christopher
Carlile, always handy and trustworthy, was put
on shore with a thousand men to attack the place
on the undefended side. The Spanish commander,
the bishop, and most of the people fled, as at
Vigo, into the mountains with their plate and
money. Carlile entered without opposition, and
flew St. George's Cross from the castle as a signal
to the fleet. Drake came in, landed the rest of
his force, and took possession. It happened to be
the 17th of November—the anniversary of the
Queen's accession—and ships and batteries, dressed
out with English flags, celebrated the occasion
with salvoes of cannon. Houses and magazines
were then searched and plundered. Wine was
found in large quantities, rich merchandise for
the Indian trade, and other valuables. Of gold
and silver nothing—it had all been removed.
Drake waited for a fortnight, hoping that the
Spaniards would treat for the ransom of the city.
When they made no sign, he marched twelve
miles inland to a village where the Governor and
the bishop were said to have taken refuge. But

the village was found deserted. The Spaniards had gone to the mountains, where it was useless to follow them, and were too proud to bargain with a pirate chief. Sant Iago was a beautifully built city, and Drake would perhaps have spared it; but a ship-boy who had strayed was found murdered and barbarously mutilated. The order was given to burn. Houses, magazines, churches, public buildings were turned to ashes, and the work being finished Drake went on, as Santa Cruz expected, for the Spanish West Indies. The Spaniards were magnificent in all that they did and touched. They built their cities in their new possessions on the most splendid models of the Old World. St. Domingo and Carthagena had their castles and cathedrals, palaces, squares, and streets, grand and solid as those at Cadiz and Seville, and raised as enduring monuments of the power and greatness of the Castilian monarchs. To these Drake meant to pay a visit. Beyond them was the Isthmus, where he had made his first fame and fortune, with Panama behind, the depôt of the Indian treasure. So far all had gone well with him. He had taken what he wanted out of

Vigo; he had destroyed Sant Iago and had not lost a man. Unfortunately he had now a worse enemy to deal with than Spanish galleons or Spanish garrisons. He was in the heat of the tropics. Yellow fever broke out and spread through the fleet. Of those who caught the infection few recovered, or recovered only to be the wrecks of themselves. It was swift in its work. In a few days more than two hundred had died. But the north-east trade blew merrily. The fleet sped on before it. In eighteen days they were in the roads at Dominica, the island of brooks and rivers and fruit. Limes and lemons and oranges were not as yet. But there were leaves and roots of the natural growth, known to the Caribs as antidotes to the fever, and the Caribs, when they learnt that the English were the Spaniards' enemies, brought them this precious remedy and taught them the use of it. The ships were washed and ventilated, and the water casks refilled. The infection seemed to have gone as suddenly as it appeared, and again all was well.

Christmas was kept at St. Kitts, which was then uninhabited. A council of war was held to

consider what should be done next.   St. Domingo
lay nearest to them.   It was the finest of all the
Spanish colonial cities.   It was the capital of the
West Indian Government, the great centre of
West Indian commerce.   In the cathedral, before
the high altar, lay Columbus and his brother
Diego.   In natural wealth no island in the world
outrivals Espinola, where the city stood.   A vast
population had collected there, far away from
harm, protected, as they supposed, by the majesty
of the mother country, the native inhabitants
almost exterminated, themselves undreaming that
any enemy could approach them from the ocean,
and therefore negligent of defence and enjoying
themselves in easy security.

Drake was to give them a new experience and
a lesson for the future.   On their way across from
St. Kitts the adventurers overhauled a small
vessel bound to the same port as they were.   From
the crew of this vessel they learnt that the
harbour at St. Domingo was formed, like so many
others in the West Indies, by a long sandspit,
acting as a natural breakwater.   The entrance
was a narrow inlet at the extremity of the spit,

and batteries had been mounted there to cover it.
To land on the outer side of the sandbank was
made impossible by the surf. There was one
sheltered point only where boats could go on
shore, but this was ten miles distant from the
town.

Ten miles was but a morning's march. Drake
went in himself in a pinnace, surveyed the
landing-place, and satisfied himself of its safety.
The plan of attack at Sant Iago was to be exactly
repeated. On New Year's Eve Christopher Carlile
was again landed with half the force in the fleet.
Drake remained with the rest, and prepared to
force the entrance of the harbour if Carlile succeeded. Their coming had been seen from the
city. The alarm had been given, and the women
and children, the money in the treasury, the con-
secrated plate, movable property of all kinds, were
sent off inland as a precaution. Of regular troops
there seem to have been none, but in so populous
a city there was no difficulty in collecting a respectable force to defend it. The hidalgos formed a
body of cavalry. The people generally were unused
to arms, but they were Spaniards and brave men,

and did not mean to leave their homes without a fight for it. Carlile lay still for the night. He marched at eight in the morning on New Year's Day, advanced leisurely, and at noon found himself in front of the wall. So far he had met no resistance, but a considerable body of horse—gentlemen and their servants chiefly—charged down on him out of the bush and out of the town. He formed into a square to receive them. They came on gallantly, but were received with pike and shot, and after a few attempts gave up and retired. Two gates were in front of Carlile, with a road to each leading through a jungle. At each gate were cannon, and the jungle was lined with musketeers. He divided his men and attacked both together. One party he led in person. The cannon opened on him, and an Englishman next to him was killed. He dashed on, leaving the Spaniards no time to reload, carried the gate at a rush, and cut his way through the streets to the great square. The second division had been equally successful, and St. Domingo was theirs except the castle, which was still untaken. Carlile's numbers were too small to occupy a large city.

He threw up barricades and fortified himself in the square for the night. Drake brought the fleet in at daybreak, and landed guns, when the castle surrendered. A messenger—a negro boy—was sent to the Governor to learn the terms which he was prepared to offer to save the city from pillage. The Spanish officers were smarting with the disgrace. One of them struck the lad through the body with a lance. He ran back bleeding to the English lines and died at Drake's feet. Sir Francis was a dangerous man to provoke. Such doings had to be promptly stopped. In the part of the town which he occupied was a monastery with a number of friars in it. The religious orders, he well knew, were the chief instigators of the policy which was maddening the world. He sent two of these friars with the provost-marshal to the spot where the boy had been struck, promptly hanged them, and then despatched another to tell the Governor that he would hang two more every day at the same place till the officer was punished. The Spaniards had long learnt to call Drake the Draque, the serpent, the devil. They feared that the devil might be a man of his word.

The offender was surrendered. It was not enough. Drake insisted that they should do justice on him themselves. The Governor found it prudent to comply, and the too hasty officer was executed.

The next point was the ransom of the city. The Spaniards still hesitating, 200 men were told off each morning to burn, while the rest searched the private houses, and palaces, and magazines. Government House was the grandest building in the New World. It was approached by broad flights of marble stairs. Great doors opened on a spacious gallery leading into a great hall, and above the portico hung the arms of Spain—a globe representing the world, a horse leaping upon it, and in the horse's mouth a scroll with the haughty motto, 'Non sufficit orbis.' Palace and scutcheon were levelled into dust by axe and gunpowder, and each day for a month the destruction went on, Drake's demands steadily growing and the unhappy Governor vainly pleading impossibility.

Vandalism, atrocity unheard of among civilised nations, dishonour to the Protestant cause, Drake deserving to swing at his own yardarm; so indignant Liberalism shrieked, and has not ceased shrieking. Let it be remembered that for fifteen years the Spaniards had been burning English seamen whenever they could catch them, plotting to kill the Queen and reduce England itself into vassaldom to the Pope. The English nation, the loyal part of it, were replying to the wild pretension by the hands of their own admiral. If Philip chose to countenance assassins, if the Holy Office chose to burn English sailors as heretics, those heretics had a right to make Spain understand that such a game was dangerous, that, as Santa Cruz had said, they had teeth and could use them.

It was found in the end that the Governor's plea of impossibility was more real than was at first believed. The gold and silver had been really carried off. All else that was valuable had been burnt or taken by the English. The destruction of a city so solidly built was tedious and difficult. Nearly half of it was blown up. The cathedral was spared, perhaps as the resting-place of Columbus. Drake had other work before him. After staying a month in undisturbed

occupation he agreed to accept 25,000 ducats as
a ransom for what was left and sailed away.

It was now February. The hot season was
coming on, when the climate would be dangerous.
There was still much to do and the time was
running short. Panama had to be left for another
opportunity. Drake's object was to deal blows
which would shake the faith of Europe in the
Spanish power. Carthagena stood next to St.
Domingo among the Spanish West Indian fortresses. The situation was strong. In 1740
Carthagena was able to beat off Vernon and a
great English fleet. But Drake's crews were in
high health and spirits, and he determined to see
what he could do with it. Surprise was no longer
to be hoped for. The alarm had spread over the
Caribbean Sea. But in their present humour
they were ready to go anywhere and dare anything,
and to Carthagena they went.

Drake's name carried terror before it. Every
non-combatant—old men, women and children—
had been cleared out before he arrived, but the
rest prepared for a smart defence. The harbour
at Carthagena was formed, as at St. Domingo

and Port Royal, by a sandspit. The spit was long, narrow, in places not fifty yards wide, and covered with prickly bush, and along this, as before, it was necessary to advance to reach the city. A trench had been cut across at the neck, and a stiff barricade built and armed with heavy guns; behind this were several hundred musketeers, while the bush was full of Indians with poisoned arrows. Pointed stakes—poisoned also—had been driven into the ground along the approaches, on which to step was death. Two large galleys, full of men, patrolled inside the bank on the harbour edge, and with these preparations the inhabitants hoped to keep the dreadful Drake from reaching them. Carlile, as before, was to do the land fighting. He was set on shore three miles down the spit. The tide is slight in those seas, but he waited till it was out, and advanced along the outer shore at low-water mark. He was thus covered by the bank from the harbour galleys, and their shots passed over him. Two squadrons of horse came out, but could do nothing to him on the broken ground. The English pushed on to the wall, scarcely losing a

man. They charged, scaled the parapets, and
drove the Spanish infantry back at point of pike.
Carlile killed their commander with his own hand.
The rest fled after a short struggle, and Drake
was master of Carthagena. Here for six weeks
he remained. The Spaniards withdrew out of
the city, and there were again parleys over the
ransom money. Courtesies were exchanged among
the officers. Drake entertained the Governor and
his suite. The Governor returned the hospitality
and received Drake and the English captains.
Drake demanded 100,000 ducats. The Spaniards
offered 30,000, and protested that they could pay
no more. The dispute might have lasted longer,
but it was cut short by the re-appearance of the
yellow fever in the fleet, this time in a deadlier
form. The Spanish offer was accepted, and Carthagena was left to its owners. It was time to
be off, for the heat was telling, and the men
began to drop with appalling rapidity. Nombre
de Dios and Panama were near and under their
lee, and Drake threw longing eyes on what, if
all else had been well, might have proved an easy
capture. But on a review of their strength, it

was found that there were but 700 fit for duty
who could be spared for the service, and a council
of war decided that a march across the Isthmus
with so small a force was too dangerous to be
ventured.   Enough had been done for glory,
enough for the political impression to be made in
Europe.   The King of Spain had been dared in
his own dominions.   Three fine Spanish cities
had been captured by storm and held to ransom.
In other aspects the success had fallen short of
expectation.   This time they had taken no
Cacafuego with a year's produce of the mines in
her hold.   The plate and coin had been carried
off, and the spoils had been in a form not easily
turned to value.   The expedition had been fitted
out by private persons to pay its own cost.   The
result in money was but 60,000*l*.   Forty thousand
had to be set aside for expenses.   There remained
but 20,000*l*. to be shared among the ships' companies.   Men and officers had entered, high and
low, without wages, on the chance of what they
might get.   The officers and owners gave a
significant demonstration of the splendid spirit
in which they had gone about their work.   They

decided to relinquish their own claims on the ransom paid for Carthagena, and bestow the same on the common seamen, 'wishing it were so much again as would be a sufficient reward for their painful endeavour.'

Thus all were well satisfied, conscious all that they had done their duty to their Queen and country. The adventurers' fleet turned homewards at the beginning of April. What men could do they had achieved. They could not fight against the pestilence of the tropics. For many days the yellow fever did its deadly work among them, and only slowly abated. They were delayed by calms and unfavourable winds. Their water ran short. They had to land again at Cape Antonio, the western point of Cuba, and sink wells to supply themselves. Drake himself, it was observed, worked with spade and bucket, like the meanest person in the whole company, always foremost where toil was to be endured or honour won, the wisest in the devising of enterprises, the calmest in danger, the first to set an example of energy in difficulties, and, above all, the firmest in maintaining order and discipline.

The fever slackened as they reached the cooler latitudes. They worked their way up the Bahama Channel, going north to avoid the trades. The French Protestants had been attempting to colonise in Florida. The Spaniards had built a fortress on the coast, to observe their settlements and, as occasion offered, cut Huguenot throats. As he passed by Drake paid this fortress a visit and wiped it out. Farther north again he was in time to save the remnant of an English settlement, rashly planted there by another brilliant servant of Queen Elizabeth.

Of all the famous Elizabethans Sir Walter Raleigh is the most romantically interesting. His splendid and varied gifts, his chequered fortunes, and his cruel end, will embalm his memory in English history. But Raleigh's great accomplishments promised more than they performed. His hand was in everything, but of work successfully completed he had less to show than others far his inferiors, to whom fortune had offered fewer opportunities. He was engaged in a hundred schemes at once, and in every one of them there was always some taint of self, some personal

ambition or private object to be gained. His
life is a record of undertakings begun in enthusiasm, maintained imperfectly, and failures in the
end. Among his other adventures he had sent
a colony to Virginia. He had imagined, or had
been led by others to believe, that there was an
Indian Court there brilliant as Montezuma's, an
enlightened nation crying to be admitted within
the charmed circle of Gloriana's subjects. His
princes and princesses proved things of air,
or mere Indian savages; and of Raleigh there
remains nothing in Virginia save the name of the
city which is called after him. The starving
survivors of his settlement on the Roanoke River
were taken on board by Drake's returning
squadron and carried home to England, where
they all arrived safely, to the glory of God, as
our pious ancestors said and meant in uncon-
ventional sincerity, on the 28th of July, 1586.

The expedition, as I have said, barely paid its
cost. In the shape of wages the officers received
nothing, and the crews but a few pounds a man;
but there was, perhaps, not one of them who was
not better pleased with the honour which he had

brought back than if he had come home loaded
with doubloons.

Startled Catholic Europe meanwhile rubbed
its eyes and began to see that the 'enterprise of
England,' as the intended invasion was called,
might not be the easy thing which the seminary
priests described it. The seminary priests had
said that so far as England was Protestant at all
it was Protestant only by the accident of its
Government, that the immense majority of the
people were Catholic at heart and were thirsting
for a return to the fold, that on the first appearance of a Spanish army of deliverance the whole
edifice which Elizabeth had raised would crumble
to the ground. I suppose it is true that if the
world had then been advanced to its present
point of progress, if there had been then recognised a Divine right to rule in the numerical
majority, even without a Spanish army the
seminary priests would have had their way.
Elizabeth's Parliaments were controlled by the
municipalities of the towns, and the towns were
Protestant. A Parliament chosen by universal
suffrage and electoral districts would have sent

Cecil and Walsingham into private life or to the scaffold, replaced the Mass in the churches, and reduced the Queen, if she had been left on the throne, into the humble servant of the Pope and Philip. It would not perhaps have lasted, but that, so far as I can judge, would have been the immediate result, and instead of a Reformation we should have had the light come in the shape of lightning. But I have often asked my Radical friends what is to be done if out of every hundred enlightened voters two-thirds will give their votes one way, but are afraid to fight, and the remaining third will not only vote but will fight too if the poll goes against them? Which has then the right to rule? I can tell them which will rule. The brave and resolute minority will rule. Plato says that if one man was stronger than all the rest of mankind he would rule all the rest of mankind. It must be so, because there is no appeal. The majority must be prepared to assert their Divine right with their right hands, or it will go the way that other Divine rights have gone before. I will not believe the world to have been so ill-constructed that there are rights which cannot be enforced. It appears to me that the true right to rule in any nation lies with those who are best and bravest, whether their numbers are large or small; and three centuries ago the best and bravest part of this English nation had determined, though they were but a third of it, that Pope and Spaniard should be no masters of theirs. Imagination goes for much in such excited times. To the imagination of Europe in the sixteenth century the power of Spain appeared irresistible if she chose to exert it. Heretic Dutchmen might rebel in a remote province, English pirates might take liberties with Spanish traders, but the Prince of Parma was making the Dutchmen feel their master at last. The pirates were but so many wasps, with venom in their stings, but powerless to affect the general tendencies of things. Except to the shrewder eyes of such men as Santa Cruz the strength of the English at sea had been left out of count in the calculations of the resources of Elizabeth's Government. Suddenly a fleet of these same pirates, sent out, unassisted by their sovereign, by the private impulse of a few indi-

viduals, had insulted the sacred soil of Spain
herself, sailed into Vigo, pillaged the churches,
taken anything that they required, and had gone
away unmolested. They had attacked, stormed,
burnt, or held to ransom three of Spain's proudest
colonial cities, and had come home unfought with.
The Catholic conspirators had to recognise that
they had a worse enemy to deal with than Puritan
controversialists or spoilt Court favourites. The
Protestant English mariners stood between them
and their prey, and had to be encountered on an
element which did not bow to popes or princes,
before Mary Stuart was to wear Elizabeth's crown
or Cardinal Allen be enthroned at Canterbury.
It was a revelation to all parties. Elizabeth
herself had not expected—perhaps had not wished
—so signal a success. War was now looked on
as inevitable. The Spanish admirals represented
that the national honour required revenge for an
injury so open and so insolent. The Pope, who
had been long goading the lethargic Philip into
action, believed that now at last he would be
compelled to move; and even Philip himself,
enduring as he was, had been roused to perceive

that intrigues and conspiracies would serve his
turn no longer. He must put out his strength
in earnest, or his own Spaniards might turn upon
him as unworthy of the crown of Isabella. Very
reluctantly he allowed the truth to be brought
home to him. He had never liked the thought
of invading England. If he conquered it, he
would not be allowed to keep it. Mary Stuart
would have to be made queen, and Mary Stuart
was part French, and might be wholly French.
The burden of the work would be thrown entirely
on his shoulders, and his own reward was to be
the Church's blessing and the approval of his
own conscience—nothing else, so far as he could
see. The Pope would recover his annates, his
Peter's pence, and his indulgence market.

If the thing was to be done, the Pope, it was
clear, ought to pay part of the cost, and this was
what the Pope did not intend to do if he could
help it. The Pope was flattering himself that
Drake's performance would compel Spain to go
to war with England whether he assisted or did
not. In this matter Philip attempted to un-
deceive his Holiness. He instructed Olivarez, his

ambassador at Rome, to tell the Pope that nothing had been yet done to him by the English which he could not overlook, and unless the Pope would come down with a handsome contribution peace he would make.   The Pope stormed and raged; he said he doubted whether Philip was a true son of the Church at all; he flung plates and dishes at the servants' heads at dinner.   He said that if he gave Philip money Philip would put it in his pocket and laugh at him.   Not one maravedi would he give till a Spanish army was actually landed on English shores, and from this resolution he was not to be moved.

To Philip it was painfully certain that if he invaded and conquered England the English Catholics would insist that he must make Mary Stuart queen.   He did not like Mary Stuart.   He disapproved of her character.   He distrusted her promises.   Spite of Jesuits and seminary priests, he believed that she was still a Frenchwoman at heart, and a bad woman besides.   Yet something he must do for the outraged honour of Castile. He concluded, in his slow way, that he would collect a fleet, the largest and best-appointed that had ever floated on the sea. He would send or lead it in person to the English Channel. He would command the situation with an overwhelming force, and then would choose some course which would be more convenient to himself than to his Holiness at Rome. On the whole he was inclined to let Elizabeth continue queen, and forget and forgive if she would put away her Walsinghams and her Drakes, and would promise to be good for the future. If she remained obstinate his great fleet would cover the passage of the Prince of Parma's army, and he would then dictate his own terms in London.

LECTURE VII

ATTACK ON CADIZ

I RECOLLECT being told when a boy, on sending in a bad translation of Horace, that I ought to remember that Horace was a man of intelligence and did not write nonsense. The same caution should be borne in mind by students of history. They see certain things done by kings and statesmen which they believe they can interpret by assuming such persons to have been knaves or idiots. Once an explanation given from the baser side of human nature, they assume that it is necessarily the right one, and they make their Horace into a fool without a misgiving that the folly may lie elsewhere. Remarkable men and women have usually had some rational motive for their conduct, which may be discovered, if we look for it with our eyes open.

Nobody has suffered more from bad translators than Elizabeth. The circumstances of Queen Elizabeth's birth, the traditions of her father, the interests of England, and the sentiments of the party who had sustained her claim to the succession, obliged her on coming to the throne to renew the separation from the Papacy. The Church of England was re-established on an Anglo-Catholic basis, which the rival factions might interpret each in their own way. To allow more than one form of public worship would have led in the heated temper of men's minds to quarrels and civil wars. But conscience might be left free under outward conformity, and those whom the Liturgy did not suit might use their own ritual in their private houses. Elizabeth and her wise advisers believed that if her subjects could be kept from fighting and killing one another, and were not exasperated by outward displays of difference, they would learn that righteousness of life was more important than orthodoxy, and to estimate at their real value the rival dogmas of theology. Had time permitted the experiment to have a fair trial, it would perhaps have succeeded, but, unhappily for the Queen and for England, the fire of controversy was still too hot under the ashes.   Protestants and Catholics had been taught to look on one another as enemies of God, and were still reluctant to take each other's hands at the bidding of an Act of Parliament. The more moderate of the Catholic laity saw no difference so great between the English service and the Mass as to force them to desert the churches where their fathers had worshipped for centuries. They petitioned the Council of Trent for permission to use the English Prayer Book; and had the Council consented, religious dissension would have dissolved at last into an innocent difference of opinion.   But the Council and the Pope had determined that there should be no compromise with heresy, and the request was refused, though it was backed by Philip's ambassador in London. The action of the Papacy obliged the Queen to leave the Administration in the hands of Protestants, on whose loyalty she could rely. As the struggle with the Reformation spread and deepened she was compelled to assist indirectly the Protestant party in France and Scotland. But

P

she still adhered to her own principle; she refused to put herself at the head of a Protestant League. She took no step without keeping open a line of retreat on a contrary policy. She had Catholics in her Privy Council who were pensioners of Spain. She filled her household with Catholics, and many a time drove Burghley distracted by listening to them at critical moments. Her constant effort was to disarm the antagonism of the adherents of the old belief, by admitting them to her confidence, and showing them that one part of her subjects was as dear to her as another.

For ten years she went on struggling. For ten years she was proudly able to say that during all that time no Catholic had suffered for his belief either in purse or person. The advanced section of the Catholic clergy was in despair. They saw the consciences of their flocks benumbed and their faith growing lukewarm. They stirred up the rebellion of the North. They persuaded Pius V. to force them to a sense of their duties by declaring Elizabeth excommunicated. They sent their missionaries through the English counties to recover sheep that were straying, and teach the sin of submission to a sovereign whom the Pope had deposed. Then had followed the Ridolfi plot, deliberately encouraged by the Pope and Spain, which had compelled the Government to tighten the reins. One conspiracy had followed another. Any means were held legitimate to rid the world of an enemy of God. The Queen's character was murdered by the foulest slanders, and a hundred daggers were sharpened to murder her person. The King of Spain had not advised the excommunication, because he knew that he would be expected to execute it, and he had other things to do. When called on to act, he and Alva said that if the English Catholics wanted Spanish help they must do something for themselves. To do the priests justice, they were brave enough. What they did, and how far they had succeeded in making the country disaffected, Father Parsons has told you in the paper which I read to you in a former lecture. Elizabeth refused to take care of herself. She would show no distrust. She would not dismiss the Catholic ladies and gentlemen from the household. She would allow no penal laws to be enforced

against Catholics as such. Repeated conspiracies
to assassinate her were detected and exposed,
but she would take no warning. She would
have no bodyguard. The utmost that she would
do was to allow the Jesuits and seminary priests,
who, by Parsons's own acknowledgment, were
sowing rebellion, to be banished the realm, and
if they persisted in remaining afterwards, to
be treated as traitors. When executions are
treated as martyrdoms, candidates will never be
wanting for the crown of glory, and the flame
only burnt the hotter. Tyburn and the quartering
knife was a horrid business, and Elizabeth sickened over it. She hated the severity which she
was compelled to exercise. Her name was defiled
with the grossest calumnies. She knew that she
might be murdered any day. For herself she was
proudly indifferent; but her death would and
must be followed by a furious civil war. She
told the Privy Council one day after some stormy
scene, that she would come back afterwards and
amuse herself with seeing the Queen of Scots
making their heads fly.

Philip was weary of it too. He had enough to

do in ruling his own dominions without quarrelling for ever with his sister-in-law. He had seen that she had subjects, few or many, who, if he struck, would strike back again. English money and English volunteers were keeping alive the war in the Netherlands. English privateers had plundered his gold ships, destroyed his commerce, and burnt his West Indian cities—all this in the interests of the Pope, who gave him fine words in plenty, but who, when called on for money to help in the English conquest, only flung about his dinner-plates. The Duke of Alva, while he was alive, and the Prince of Parma, who commanded in the Netherlands in Alva's place, advised peace if peace could be had on reasonable terms. If Elizabeth would consent to withdraw her help from the Netherlands, and would allow the English Catholics the tacit toleration with which her reign had begun, they were of opinion, and Philip was of opinion too, that it would be better to forgive Drake and St. Domingo, abandon Mary Stuart and the seminary priests, and meddle no more with English internal politics.

Tired with a condition which was neither war

nor peace, tired with hanging traitors and the endless problem of her sister of Scotland, Elizabeth saw no reason for refusing offers which would leave her in peace for the rest of her own life. Philip, it was said, would restore the Mass in the churches in Holland. She might stipulate for such liberty of conscience to the Holland Protestants as she was herself willing to allow the English Catholics. She saw no reason why she should insist on a liberty of public worship which she had herself forbidden at home. She did not see why the Hollanders should be so precise about hearing Mass. She said she would rather hear a thousand Masses herself than have on her conscience the crimes committed for the Mass or against it. She would not have her realm in perpetual torment for Mr. Cecil's brothers in Christ.

This was Elizabeth's personal feeling. It could not be openly avowed. The States might then surrender to Philip in despair, and obtain better securities for their political liberties than she was ready to ask for them. They might then join the Spaniards and become her mortal enemies. But she had a high opinion of her own statecraft.

Her Catholic friends assured her that, once at peace with Philip, she would be safe from all the world. At this moment accident revealed suddenly another chasm which was opening unsuspected at her feet.

Both Philip and she were really wishing for peace. A treaty of peace between the Catholic King and an excommunicated princess would end the dream of a Catholic revolution in England. If the English peers and gentry saw the censures of the Church set aside so lightly by the most orthodox prince in Europe, Parsons and his friends would preach in vain to them the obligation of rebellion. If this deadly negotiation was to be broken off, a blow must be struck, and struck at once. There was not a moment to be lost.

The enchanted prisoner at Tutbury was the sleeping and waking dream of Catholic chivalry. The brave knight who would slay the dragon, deliver Mary Stuart, and place her on the usurper's throne, would outdo Orlando or St. George, and be sung of for ever as the noblest hero who had ever wielded brand or spear. Many

a young British heart had thrilled with hope that
for him the enterprise was reserved. One of these
was a certain Anthony Babington, a gentleman
of some fortune in Derbyshire. A seminary priest
named Ballard, excited, like the rest, by the need
of action, and anxious to prevent the peace, fell
in with this Babington, and thought he had
found the man for his work. Elizabeth dead
and Mary Stuart free, there would be no more
talk of peace. A plot was easily formed. Half
a dozen gentlemen, five of them belonging to or
connected with Elizabeth's own household, were
to shoot or stab her and escape in the confusion;
Babington was to make a dash on Mary Stuart's
prison-house and carry her off to some safe place;
while Ballard undertook to raise the Catholic
peers and have her proclaimed queen. Elizabeth
once removed, it was supposed that they would
not hesitate. Parma would bring over the
Spanish army from Dunkirk. The Protestants
would be paralysed. All would be begun and
ended in a few weeks or even days. The Catholic
religion would be re-established and the hated
heresy would be trampled out for ever. Mary

Stuart had been consulted and had enthusiastically agreed.

This interesting lady had been lately profuse
in her protestations of a desire for reconciliation
with her dearest sister.   Elizabeth had almost
believed her sincere.   Sick of the endless trouble
with Mary Stuart and her pretensions and schemings, she had intended that the Scotch queen
should be included in the treaty with Philip,
with an implied recognition of her right to succeed to the English throne after Elizabeth's death.
It had been necessary, however, to ascertain in
some way whether her protestations were sincere.
A secret watch had been kept over her correspondence, and Babington's letters and her own
answers had fallen into Walsingham's hands.
There it all was in her own cipher, the key to
which had been betrayed by the carelessness of a
confederate.   The six gentlemen who were to
have rewarded Elizabeth's confidence by killing
her were easily recognised.   They were seized,
with Babington and Ballard, when they imagined
themselves on the eve of their triumph.   Babington flinched and confessed, and they were all

hanged. Mary Stuart herself had outworn compassion. Twice already on the discovery of her earlier plots the House of Commons had petitioned for her execution. For this last piece of treachery she was tried at Fotheringay before a commission of Peers and Privy Councillors. She denied her letters, but her complicity was proved beyond a doubt. Parliament was called, and a third time insisted that the long drama should now be ended and loyal England be allowed to breathe in peace. Elizabeth signed the warrant. France, Spain, any other power in the world would have long since made an end of a competitor so desperate and so incurable. Torn by many feelings— natural pity, dread of the world's opinion— Elizabeth paused before ordering the warrant to be executed. If nothing had been at stake but her own life, she would have left the lady to weave fresh plots and at last, perhaps, to succeed. If the nation's safety required an end to be made with her, she felt it hard that the duty should be thrown on herself. Where were all those eager champions who had signed the Association Bond, who had talked so loudly? Could none of them

be found to recollect their oaths and take the law
into their own hands?

Her Council, Burghley, and the rest, knowing
her disposition and feeling that it was life or
death to English liberty, took the responsibility
on themselves. They sent the warrant down to
Fotheringay at their own risk, leaving their
mistress to deny, if she pleased, that she had
meant it to be executed; and the wild career of
Mary Stuart ended on the scaffold.

They knew what they were immediately
doing. They knew that if treason had a meaning Mary Stuart had brought her fate upon herself. They did not, perhaps, realise the full
effects that were to follow, or that with Mary
Stuart had vanished the last serious danger of
a Catholic insurrection in England; or perhaps
they did realise it, and this was what decided
them to act.

I cannot dwell on this here. As long as there
was a Catholic princess of English blood to succeed to the throne, the allegiance of the Catholics
to Elizabeth had been easily shaken. If she was
spared now, every one of them would look on her

as their future sovereign. To overthrow Elizabeth might mean the loss of national independence. The Queen of Scots gone, they were paralysed by divided counsels, and love of country proved stronger than their creed.

What concerns us specially at present is the effect on the King of Spain. The reluctance of Philip to undertake the English enterprise (the 'empresa,' as it was generally called) had arisen from a fear that when it was accomplished he would lose the fruit of his labours. He could never assure himself that if he placed Mary Stuart on the throne she would not become eventually French. He now learnt that she had bequeathed to himself her claims on the English succession. He had once been titular King of England. He had pretensions of his own, as in the descent from Edward III. The Jesuits, the Catholic enthusiasts throughout Europe, assured him that if he would now take up the cause in earnest, he might make England a province of Spain. There were still difficulties. He might hope that the English Catholic laity would accept him, but he could not be sure of it.

He could not be sure that he would have the
support of the Pope. He continued, as the
Conde de Feria said scornfully of him, 'meando
en vado,' a phrase which I cannot translate; it
meant hesitating when he ought to act. But he
saw, or thought he saw, that he could now take a
stronger attitude towards Elizabeth as a claimant
to her throne. If the treaty of peace was to go
forward, he could raise his terms. He could insist on the restoration of the Catholic religion in
England. The States of the Low Countries had
made over five of their strongest towns to Elizabeth as the price of her assistance. He could
insist on her restoring them, not to the States,
but to himself. Could she be brought to consent
to such an act of perfidy, Parma and he both
felt that the power would then be gone from
her, as effectually as Samson's when his locks
were clipped by the harlot, and they could leave
her then, if it suited them, on a throne which
would have become a pillory—for the finger of
scorn to point at.

With such a view before him it was more than
ever necessary for Philip to hurry forward the

preparations which he had already com-
menced. The more formidable he could make
himself, the better able he would be to frighten
Elizabeth into submission.

Every dockyard in Spain was set to work,
building galleons and collecting stores. Santa
Cruz would command. Philip was himself more
resolved than ever to accompany the expedition
in person and dictate from the English Channel
the conditions of the pacification of Europe.

Secrecy was no longer attempted—indeed,
was no longer possibe. All Latin Christendom
was palpitating with expectation. At Lisbon, at
Cadiz, at Barcelona, at Naples, the shipwrights
were busy night and day. The sea was covered
with vessels freighted with arms and provisions
streaming to the mouth of the Tagus. Catholic
volunteers from all nations flocked into the
Peninsula, to take a share in the mighty move-
ment which was to decide the fate of the world,
and bishops, priests, and monks were set praying
through the whole Latin Communion that
Heaven would protect its own cause.

Meantime the negotiations for peace con-

tinued, and Elizabeth, strange to say, persisted
in listening. She would not see what was plain
to all the world besides. The execution of the
Queen of Scots lay on her spirit and threw her
back into the obstinate humour which had made
Walsingham so often despair of her safety. For
two months after that scene at Fotheringay she
had refused to see Burghley, and would consult
no one but Sir James Crofts and her Spanish-
tempered ladies. She knew that Spain now
intended that she should betray the towns in the
Low Countries, yet she was blind to the infamy
which it would bring upon her. She left her
troops there without their wages to shiver into
mutiny. She named commissioners, with Sir
James Crofts at their head, to go to Ostend and
treat with Parma, and if she had not resolved on
an act of treachery she at least played with the
temptation, and persuaded herself that if she
chose to make over the towns to Philip, she would
be only restoring them to their lawful owner.

Burghley and Walsingham, you can see from
their letters, believed now that Elizabeth had
ruined herself at last. Happily her moods were

variable as the weather. She was forced to see
the condition to which she had reduced her
affairs in the Low Countries by the appearance of
a number of starving wretches who had deserted
from the garrisons there and had come across to
clamour for their pay at her own palace gates.
If she had no troops in the field but a mutinous
and starving rabble, she might get no terms at
all. It might be well to show Philip that on one
element at least she could still be dangerous.
She had lost nothing by the bold actions of
Drake and the privateers. With half a heart she
allowed Drake to fit them out again, take the
Buonaventura, a ship of her own, to carry his flag,
and go down to the coast of Spain and see what
was going on. He was not to do too much. She
sent a vice-admiral with him, in the *Lion,* to be
a check on over-audacity. Drake knew how to
deal with embarrassing vice-admirals. His own
adventurers would sail, if he ordered, to the
Mountains of the Moon, and be quite certain that
it was the right place to go to. Once under way
and on the blue water he would go his own
course and run his own risks. Cadiz Harbour

was thronged with transports, provision ships, powder vessels—a hundred sail of them—many of a thousand tons and over, loading with stores for the Armada. There were thirty sail of adventurers, the smartest ships afloat on the ocean, and sailed by the smartest seamen that ever handled rope or tiller. Something might be done at Cadiz if he did not say too much about it. The leave had been given to him to go, but he knew by experience, and Burghley again warned him, that it might, and probably would, be revoked if he waited too long. The moment was his own, and he used it. He was but just in time. Before his sails were under the horizon a courier galloped into Plymouth with orders that under no condition was he to enter port or haven of the King of Spain, or injure Spanish subjects. What else was he going out for? He had guessed how it would be. Comedy or earnest he could not tell. If earnest, some such order would be sent after him, and he had not an instant to lose.

He sailed on the morning of the 12th of April. Off Ushant he fell in with a north-west gale, and

he flew on, spreading every stitch of canvas which
his spars would bear. In five days he was at Cape
St. Vincent. On the 18th he had the white
houses of Cadiz right in front of him, and could
see for himself the forests of masts from the
ships and transports with which the harbour was
choked. Here was a chance for a piece of
service if there was courage for the venture.
He signalled for his officers to come on board
the *Buonaventura*. There before their eyes was,
if not the Armada itself, the materials which
were to fit the Armada for the seas. Did they
dare to go in with him and destroy them ? There
were batteries at the harbour mouth, but Drake's
mariners had faced Spanish batteries at St.
Domingo and Carthagena and had not found them
very formidable. Go in ? Of course they would.
Where Drake would lead the corsairs of Plymouth
were never afraid to follow. The vice-admiral
pleaded danger to her Majesty's ships. It was
not the business of an English fleet to be particular about danger. Straight in they went with a
fair wind and a flood tide, ran past the batteries
and under a storm of shot, to which they did not

trouble themselves to wait to reply. The poor
vice-admiral followed reluctantly in the *Lion*. A
single shot hit the *Lion*, and he edged away out
of range, anchored, and drifted to sea again with
the ebb. But Drake and all the rest dashed on,
sank the guardship—a large galleon—and sent
flying a fleet of galleys which ventured too near
them and were never seen again.

Further resistance there was none—absolutely
none. The crews of the store ships escaped in
their boats to land. The governor of Cadiz, the
same Duke of Medina Sidonia who the next year
was to gain a disastrous immortality, fled 'like a
tall gentleman' to raise troops and prevent Drake
from landing. Drake had no intention of landing.
At his extreme leisure he took possession of the
Spanish shipping, searched every vessel, and
carried off everything that he could use. He detained as prisoners the few men that he found on
board, and then, after doing his work deliberately
and completely, he set the hulls on fire, cut the
cables, and left them to drive on the rising tide
under the walls of the town—a confused mass of
blazing ruin. On the 12th of April he had sailed

from Plymouth; on the 19th he entered Cadiz
Harbour; on the 1st of May he passed out again
without the loss of a boat or a man. He said in
jest that he had singed the King of Spain's beard
for him. In sober prose he had done the King
of Spain an amount of damage which a million
ducats and a year's labour would imperfectly
replace. The daring rapidity of the enterprise
astonished Spain, and astonished Europe more
than the storm of the West Indian towns. The
English had long teeth, as Santa Cruz had told
Philip's council, and the teeth would need drawing
before Mass would be heard again at Westminster.
The Spaniards were a gallant race, and a dashing
exploit, though at their own expense, could be
admired by the countrymen of Cervantes. 'So
praised,' we read, 'was Drake for his valour
among them, that they said that if he was not a
Lutheran there would not be the like of him in
the world.' A Court lady was invited by the King
to join a party on a lake near Madrid. The lady
replied that she dared not trust herself on the
water with his Majesty lest Sir Francis Drake
should have her.

Drake might well be praised. But Drake would have been the first to divide the honour with the comrades who were his arm and hand. Great admirals and generals do not win their battles single-handed like the heroes of romance. Orders avail only when there are men to execute them. Not a captain, not an officer who served under Drake, ever flinched or blundered. Never was such a school for seamen as that twenty years' privateering war between the servants of the Pope and the West-country Protestant adventurers. Those too must be remembered who built and rigged the ships in which they sailed and fought their battles. We may depend upon it that there was no dishonesty in con-tractors, no scamping of the work in the yards where the Plymouth rovers were fitted out for sea. Their hearts were in it; they were soldiers of a common cause.

Three weeks had sufficed for Cadiz. No order for recall had yet arrived. Drake had other plans before him, and the men were in high spirits and ready for anything. A fleet of Spanish men-of-war was expected round from the Mediterranean.

He proposed to stay for a week or two in the neighbourhood of the Straits, in the hope of falling in with them. He wanted fresh water, too, and had to find it somewhere.

Before leaving Cadiz Roads he had to decide what to do with his prisoners. Many English were known to be in the hands of the Holy Office working in irons as galley slaves. He sent in a pinnace to propose an exchange, and had to wait some days for an answer. At length, after a reference to Lisbon, the Spanish authorities replied that they had no English prisoners. If this was true those they had must have died of barbarous usage; and after a consultation with his officers Sir Francis sent in word that for the future such prisoners as they might take would be sold to the Moors, and the money applied to the redemption of English captives in other parts of the world.

Water was the next point. There were springs at Faro, with a Spanish force stationed there to guard them. Force or no force, water was to be had. The boats were sent on shore. The boats' crews stormed the forts and filled the casks. The vice-admiral again lifted up his voice. The Queen had ordered that there was to be no landing on Spanish soil. At Cadiz the order had been observed. There had been no need to land. Here at Faro there had been direct defiance of her Majesty's command. He became so loud in his clamours that Drake found it necessary to lock him up in his own cabin, and at length to send him home with his ship to complain. For himself, as the expected fleet from the Straits did not appear, and as he had shaken off his troublesome second in command, he proceeded leisurely up the coast, intending to look in at Lisbon and see for himself how things were going on there. All along as he went he fell in with traders loaded with supplies for the use of the Armada. All these he destroyed as he advanced, and at length found himself under the purple hills of Cintra and looking up into the Tagus. There lay gathered together the strength of the fighting naval force of Spain—fifty great galleons, already arrived, the largest war-ships which then floated on the ocean. Santa Cruz, the best officer in the Spanish navy, was himself in the town and in

command. To venture a repetition of the Cadiz
exploit in the face of such odds seemed too
desperate even for Drake, but it was one of those
occasions when the genius of a great commander
sees more than ordinary eyes. He calculated,
and, as was proved afterwards, calculated rightly,
that the galleons would be half manned, or
not manned at all, and crowded with landsmen
bringing on board the stores. Their sides as
they lay would be choked with hulks and lighters.
They would be unable to get their anchors up,
set their canvas, or stir from their moorings.
Daring as Drake was known to be, no one would
expect him to go with so small a force into the
enemy's stronghold, and there would be no preparations to meet him. He could count upon the
tides. The winds at that season of the year were
fresh and steady, and could be counted on also to
take him in or out; there was sea room in the
river for such vessels as the adventures' to manœuvre and to retreat if overmatched. Rash as
such an enterprise might seem to an unprofessional
eye, Drake certainly thought of it, perhaps had
meant to try it in some form or other and so make

an end of the Spanish invasion of England. He could not venture without asking first for his mistress's permission. He knew her nature. He knew that his services at Cadiz would outweigh his disregard of her orders, and that so far he had nothing to fear; but he knew also that she was still hankering after peace, and that without her leave he must do nothing to make peace impossible. There is a letter from him to the Queen, written when he was lying off Lisbon, very characteristic of the time and the man.

Nelson or Lord St. Vincent did not talk much of expecting supernatural assistance. If they had we should suspect them of using language conventionally which they would have done better to leave alone. Sir Francis Drake, like his other great contemporaries, believed that he was engaged in a holy cause, and was not afraid or ashamed to say so. His object was to protest against a recall in the flow of victory. The Spaniards, he said, were but mortal men. They were enemies of the Truth, upholders of Dagon's image, which had fallen in other days before the Ark, and would fall again if boldly defied. So long as he

had ships that would float, and there was food on
board them for the men to eat, he entreated her
to let him stay and strike whenever a chance was
offered him. The continuing to the end yielded
the true glory. When men were serving religion
and their country, a merciful God, it was likely,
would give them victory, and Satan and his angels
should not prevail.

All in good time. Another year and Drake
would have the chance he wanted. For the
moment Satan had prevailed—Satan in the shape
of Elizabeth's Catholic advisers. Her answer
came. It was warm and generous. She did not,
could not, blame him for what he had done so
far, but she desired him to provoke the King of
Spain no further. The negotiations for peace
had opened, and must not be interfered with.

This prohibition from the Queen prevented,
perhaps, what would have been the most remarkable exploit in English naval history. As matters
stood it would have been perfectly possible for
Drake to have gone into the Tagus, and if he
could not have burnt the galleons he could certainly have come away unhurt. He had guessed

their condition with entire correctness. The
ships were there, but the ships' companies were
not on board them. Santa Cruz himself admitted
that if Drake had gone in he could have himself
done nothing 'por falta de gente' (for want of
men). And Drake undoubtedly would have gone,
and would have done something with which all
the world would have rung, but for the positive
command of his mistress. He lingered in the
roads at Cintra, hoping that Santa Cruz would
come out and meet him. All Spain was clamour-
ing at Santa Cruz's inaction. Philip wrote to
stir the old admiral to energy. He must not
allow himself to be defied by a squadron of insolent rovers. He must chase them off the coast
or destroy them. Santa Cruz needed no stirring.
Santa Cruz, the hero of a hundred fights, was
chafing at his own impotence; but he was obliged
to tell his master that if he wished to have
service out of his galleons he must provide
crews to handle them, and they must rot at
their anchors till he did. He told him, more-
over, that it was time for him to exert himself
in earnest. If he waited much longer, England

would have grown too strong for him to deal
with.

In strict obedience Drake ought now to have
gone home, but the campaign had brought so far
more glory than prize-money. His comrades required some consolation for their disappointment
at Lisbon. The theory of these armaments of
the adventurers was that the cost should be paid
somehow by the enemy, and he could be assured
that if he brought back a prize or two in which
she could claim a share the Queen would not call
him to a very strict account. Homeward-bound
galleons or merchantmen were to be met with
occasionally at the Azores. On leaving Lisbon
Drake headed away to St. Michael's, and his
lucky star was still in the ascendant.

As if sent on purpose for him, the *San Philip*,
a magnificent caraque from the Indies, fell
straight into his hands, 'so richly loaded,' it was
said, 'that every man in the fleet counted his
fortune made.' There was no need to wait for
more. It was but two months since Drake had
sailed from Plymouth. He could now go home
after a cruise of which the history of his own or

any other country had never presented the like. He had struck the King of Spain in his own stronghold. He had disabled the intended Armada for one season at least. He had picked up a prize by the way and as if by accident, worth half a million, to pay his expenses, so that he had cost nothing to his mistress, and had brought back a handsome present for her. I doubt if such a naval estimate was ever presented to an English House of Commons. Above all he had taught the self-confident Spaniard to be afraid of him, and he carried back his poor comrades in such a glow of triumph that they would have fought Satan and all his angels with Drake at their head.

Our West-country annals still tell how the country people streamed down in their best clothes to see the great *San Philip* towed into Dartmouth Harbour. English Protestantism was no bad cable for the nation to ride by in those stormy times, and deserves to be honourably remembered in a School of History at an English University.

LECTURE VIII

SAILING OF THE ARMADA

PEACE or war between Spain and England,
that was now the question, with a prospect
of securing the English succession for himself or
one of his daughters. With the whole Spanish
nation smarting under the indignity of the burning of the ships at Cadiz, Philip's warlike ardour
had warmed into something like fire. He had
resolved at any rate, if he was to forgive his
sister-in-law at all, to insist on more than toleration for the Catholics in England. He did not
contemplate as even possible that the English
privateers, however bold or dexterous, could resist
such an armament as he was preparing to lead
to the Channel. The Royal Navy, he knew very
well, did not exceed twenty-five ships of all sorts
and sizes. The adventurers might be equal to

sudden daring actions, but would and must be crushed by such a fleet as was being fitted out at Lisbon. He therefore, for himself, meant to demand that the Catholic religion should be restored to its complete and exclusive superiority, and certain towns in England were to be made over to be garrisoned by Spanish troops as securities for Elizabeth's good behaviour. As often happens with irresolute men, when they have once been forced to a decision they are as too hasty as before they were too slow. After Drake had retired from Lisbon the King of Spain sent orders to the Prince of Parma not to wait for the arrival of the Armada, but to cross the Channel immediately with the Flanders army, and bring Elizabeth to her knees. Parma had more sense than his master. He represented that he could not cross without a fleet to cover his passage. His transport barges would only float in smooth water, and whether the water was smooth or rough they could be sent to the bottom by half a dozen English cruisers from the Thames. Supposing him to have landed, either in Thanet or other spot, he reminded Philip that he could not

have at most more than 25,000 men with him.
The English militia were in training. The Jesuits
said they were disaffected, but the Jesuits might
be making a mistake. He might have to fight
more than one battle. He would have to leave
detachments as he advanced to London, to cover
his communications, and a reverse would be fatal.
He would obey if his Majesty persisted, but he
recommended Philip to continue to amuse the
English with the treaty till the Armada was
ready, and, in evident consciousness that the
enterprise would be harder than Philip imagined,
he even gave it as his own opinion still (notwithstanding Cadiz), that if Elizabeth would surrender
the cautionary towns in Flanders to Spain, and
would grant the English Catholics a fair degree
of liberty, it would be Philip's interest to make
peace at once without stipulating for further
terms. He could make a new war if he wished
at a future time, when circumstances might be
more convenient and the Netherlands revolt
subdued.

To such conditions as these it seemed that
Elizabeth was inclining to consent. The towns

had been trusted to her keeping by the Nether-
landers. To give them up to the enemy to make
better conditions for herself would be an infamy
so great as to have disgraced Elizabeth for ever;
yet she would not see it. She said the towns
belonged to Philip and she would only be restoring his own to him. Burghley bade her, if she
wanted peace, send back Drake to the Azores
and frighten Philip for his gold ships. She was
in one of her ungovernable moods. Instead of
sending out Drake again she ordered her own
fleet to be dismantled and laid up at Chatham,
and she condescended to apologise to Parma for
the burning of the transports at Cadiz as done
against her orders.

This was in December 1587, only five months
before the Armada sailed from Lisbon. Never
had she brought herself and her country so near
ruin. The entire safety of England rested at
that moment on the adventurers, and on the
adventurers alone.

Meanwhile, with enormous effort the destruction at Cadiz had been repaired. The great fleet
was pushed on, and in February Santa Cruz

reported himself almost ready. Santa Cruz and
Philip, however, were not in agreement as to
what should be done. Santa Cruz was a fighting
admiral, Philip was not a fighting king. He
changed his mind as often as Elizabeth. Hot
fits varied with cold. His last news from England
led him to hope that fighting would not be
wanted. The Commissioners were sitting at
Ostend. On one side there were the formal
negotiations, in which the surrender of the towns
was not yet treated as an open question. Had
the States been aware that Elizabeth was even
in thought entertaining it, they would have made
terms instantly on their own account and left
her alone in the cold. Besides this, there was a
second negotiation underneath, carried on by
private agents, in which the surrender was to
be the special condition. These complicated
schemings Parma purposely protracted, to keep
Elizabeth in false security. She had not deliberately intended to give up the towns. At the last
moment she would have probably refused, unless
the States themselves consented to it as part of
a general settlement. But she was playing with

the idea. The States, she thought, were too obstinate. Peace would be good for them, and she said she might do them good if she pleased, whether they liked it or not.

Parma was content that she should amuse herself with words and neglect her defences by sea and land. By the end of February Santa Cruz was ready. A northerly wind blows strong down the coast of Portugal in the spring months, and he meant to be off before it set in, before the end of March at latest. Unfortunately for Spain, Santa Cruz fell ill at the last moment—ill, it was said, with anxiety. Santa Cruz knew well enough what Philip would not know—that the expedition would be no holiday parade. He had reason enough to be anxious if Philip was to accompany him and tie his hands and embarrass him. Anyway, Santa Cruz died after a few days' illness. The sailing had to be suspended till a new commander could be decided on, and in the choice which Philip made he gave a curious proof of what he intended the expedition to do. He did not really expect or wish for any serious fighting. He wanted to be sovereign of England again, with the assent of the English Catholics. He did not mean, if he could help it, to irritate the national pride by force and conquest. While Santa Cruz lived, Spanish public opinion would not allow him to be passed over. Santa Cruz must command, and Philip had resolved to go with him, to prevent too violent proceedings. Santa Cruz dead, he could find someone who would do what he was told, and his own presence would no longer be necessary.

The Duke of Medina Sidonia, named El Bueno, or the Good, was a grandee of highest rank. He was enormously rich, fond of hunting and shooting, a tolerable rider, for the rest a harmless creature getting on to forty, conscious of his defects, but not aware that so great a prince had any need to mend them; without vanity, without ambition, and most happy when lounging in his orange gardens at San Lucan. Of active service he had seen none. He was Captain-General of Andalusia, and had run away from Cadiz when Drake came into the harbour; but that was all. To his astonishment and to his dismay he learnt that it was on him that the choice had fallen to be the Lord High Admiral of Spain and commander of the so much talked of expedition to England. He protested his unfitness. He said that he was no seaman; that he knew nothing of fighting by sea or land; that if he ventured out in a boat he was always sick; that he had never seen the English Channel; and that, as to politics, he neither knew anything nor cared anything about them. In short, he had not one qualification which such a post required.

Philip liked his modesty; but in fact the Duke's defects were his recommendations. He would obey his instructions, would not fight unless it was necessary, and would go into no rash adventures. All that Philip wanted him to do was to find the Prince of Parma, and act as Parma should bid him. As to seamanship, he would have the best officers in the navy under him; and for a second in command he should have Don Diego de Valdez, a cautious, silent, sullen old sailor, a man after Philip's own heart.

Doubting, hesitating, the Duke repaired to Lisbon. There he was put in better heart by a nun, who said Our Lady had sent her to promise

him success. Every part of the service was new
to him. He was a fussy, anxious little man; set
himself to inquire into everything, to meddle with
things which he could not understand and had
better have left alone. He ought to have left
details to the responsible heads of departments.
He fancied that in a week or two he could look
himself into everything. There were 130 ships,
8,000 seamen, 19,000 Spanish infantry, with
gentlemen volunteers, officers, priests, surgeons,
galley slaves—at least 3,000 more—provisioned
for six months. Then there were the ships' stores,
arms small and great, powder, spars, cordage,
canvas, and such other million necessities as ships
on service need. The whole of this the poor
Duke took on himself to examine into, and, as he
could not understand what he saw, and knew not
what to look at, nothing was examined into at all.
Everyone's mind was, in fact, so much absorbed
by the spiritual side of the thing that they could
not attend to vulgar commonplaces. Don Quixote,
when he set out on his expedition, and forgot
money and a change of linen, was not in a state
of wilder exaltation than Catholic Europe at the

sailing of the Armada. Every noble family in
Spain had sent one or other of its sons to fight
for Christ and Our Lady.

For three years the stream of prayer had been
ascending from church, cathedral, or oratory.
The King had emptied his treasury. The hidalgo
and the tradesman had offered their contributions.
The crusade against the Crescent itself had not
kindled a more intense or more sacred enthusiasm.
All pains were taken to make the expedition
spiritually worthy of its purpose. No impure
thing, specially no impure woman, was to approach
the yards or ships. Swearing, quarrelling, gamb-
ling, were prohibited under terrible penalties. The
galleons were named after the apostles and saints
to whose charge they were committed, and every
seaman and soldier confessed and communicated
on going on board. The shipboys at sunrise
were to sing their Buenos Dias at the foot of the
mainmast, and their Ave Maria as the sun sank
into the ocean. On the Imperial banner were
embroidered the figures of Christ and His Mother,
and as a motto the haughty 'Plus Ultra' of
Charles V. was replaced with the more pious

aspiration, ' Exsurge, Deus, et vindica causam tuam.'

Nothing could be better if the more vulgar necessities had been looked to equally well. Unluckily, Medina Sidonia had taken the inspection of these on himself, and Medina Sidonia was unable to correct the information which any rascal chose to give him.

At length, at the end of April, he reported himself satisfied. The banner was blessed in the cathedral, men and stores all on board, and the Invincible Armada prepared to go upon its way. No wonder Philip was confident. A hundred and thirty galleons, from 1,300 to 700 tons, 30,000 fighting men, besides slaves and servants, made up a force which the world might well think invincible. The guns were the weakest part. There were twice as many as the English ; but they were for the most part nine and six pounders, and with but fifty rounds to each. The Spaniards had done their sea fighting hitherto at close range, grappling and trusting to musketry. They were to receive a lesson about this before the summer was over. But Philip himself meanwhile expected evidently that he would meet with no opposition. Of priests he had provided 180; of surgeons and surgeons' assistants eighty-five only for the whole fleet.

In the middle of May he sent down his last orders. The Duke was not to seek a battle. If he fell in with Drake he was to take no notice of him, but thank God, as Dogberry said to the watchman, that he was rid of a knave. He was to go straight to the North Foreland, there anchor and communicate with Parma. The experienced admirals who had learnt their trade under Santa Cruz—Martinez de Recalde, Pedro de Valdez, Miguel de Oquendo—strongly urged the securing Plymouth or the Isle of Wight on their way up Channel. This had evidently been Santa Cruz's own design, and the only rational one to have followed. Philip did not see it. He did not believe it would prove necessary; but as to this and as to fighting he left them, as he knew he must do, a certain discretion.

The Duke then, flying the sacred banner on the *San Martin*, dropped down the Tagus on the 14th of May, followed by the whole fleet. The

San Martin had been double-timbered with oak, to keep the shot out. He liked his business no better. In vain he repeated to himself that it was God's cause. God would see they came to no harm. He was no sooner in the open sea than he found no cause, however holy, saved men from the consequences of their own blunders. They were late out, and met the north trade wind, as Santa Cruz had foretold.

They drifted to leeward day by day till they had dropped down to Cape St. Vincent. Infinite pains had been taken with the spiritual state of everyone on board. The carelessness or roguery of contractors and purveyors had not been thought of. The water had been taken in three months before. It was found foul and stinking. The salt beef, the salt pork, and fish were putrid, the bread full of maggots and cockroaches. Cask was opened after cask. It was the same story everywhere. They had to be all thrown overboard. In the whole fleet there was not a sound morsel of food but biscuit and dried fruit. The men went down in hundreds with dysentery. The Duke bewailed his fate as innocently as Sancho

Panza. He hoped God would help. He had wished no harm to anybody. He had left his home and his family to please the King, and he trusted the King would remember it. He wrote piteously for fresh stores, if the King would not have them all perish. The admirals said they could go no further without fresh water. All was dismay and confusion. The wind at last fell round south, and they made Finisterre. It then came on to blow, and they were scattered. The Duke with half the fleet crawled into Corunna, the crews scarce able to man the yards and trying to desert in shoals.

The missing ships dropped in one by one, but a week passed and a third of them were still absent. Another despairing letter went off from the Duke to his master. He said that he concluded from their misfortunes that God disapproved of the expedition, and that it had better be abandoned. Diego Florez was of the same opinion. The stores were worthless, he said. The men were sick and out of heart. Nothing could be done that season.

It was not by flinching at the first sight of

difficulty that the Spaniards had become masters of half the world. The old comrades of Santa Cruz saw nothing in what had befallen them beyond a common accident of sea life. To abandon at the first check an enterprise undertaken with so much pretence, they said, would be cowardly and dishonourable. Ships were not lost because they were out of sight. Fresh meat and bread could be taken on board from Corunna. They could set up a shore hospital for the sick. The sickness was not dangerous. There had been no deaths. A little energy and all would be well again. Pedro de Valdez despatched a courier to Philip to entreat him not to listen to the Duke's croakings. Philip returned a speedy answer telling the Duke not to be frightened at shadows.

There was nothing, in fact, really to be alarmed at. Fresh water took away the dysentery. Fresh food was brought in from the country. Galician seamen filled the gaps made by the deserters. The ships were laid on shore and scraped and tallowed. Tents were pitched on an island in the harbour, with altars and priests, and everyone confessed again and received the Sacrament.

'This,' wrote the Duke, 'is great riches and a precious jewel, and all now are well content and cheerful.' The scattered flock had reassembled. Damages were all repaired, and the only harm had been loss of time. Once more, on the 23rd of July, the Armada in full numbers was under way for England and streaming across the Bay of Biscay with a fair wind for the mouth of the Channel.

Leaving the Duke for the moment, we must now glance at the preparations made in England to receive him. It might almost be said that there were none at all. The winter months had been wild and changeable, but not so wild and not so fluctuating as the mind of England's mistress. In December her fleet had been paid off at Chatham. The danger of leaving the country without any regular defence was pressed on her so vehemently that she consented to allow part of the ships to be recommissioned. The *Revenge* was given to Drake. He and Howard, the Lord Admiral, were to have gone with a mixed squadron from the Royal Navy and the adventurers down to the Spanish coast. In every

loyal subject there had long been but one opinion,
that a good open war was the only road to an
honourable peace. The open war, they now
trusted, was come at last. But the hope was
raised only to be disappointed. With the news
of Santa Cruz's death came a report which
Elizabeth greedily believed, that the Armada
was dissolving and was not coming at all. Sir
James Crofts sang the usual song that Drake and
Howard wanted war, because war was their trade.
She recalled her orders. She said that she was
assured of peace in six weeks, and that beyond
that time the services of the fleet would not be
required. Half the men engaged were to be
dismissed at once to save their pay. Drake and
Lord Henry Seymour might cruise with four
or five of the Queen's ships between Plymouth
and the Solent. Lord Howard was to remain in
the Thames with the rest. I know not whether
swearing was interdicted in the English navy as
well as in the Spanish, but I will answer for it
that Howard did not spare his language when
this missive reached him. 'Never,' he said 'since
England was England was such a stratagem

made to deceive us as this treaty. We have not hands left to carry the ships back to Chatham. We are like bears tied to a stake; the Spaniards may come to worry us like dogs, and we cannot hurt them.'

It was well for England that she had other defenders than the wildly managed navy of the Queen. Historians tell us how the gentlemen of the coast came out in their own vessels to meet the invaders. Come they did, but who were they? Ships that could fight the Spanish galleons were not made in a day or a week. They were built already. They were manned by loyal subjects, the business of whose lives had been to meet the enemies of their land and faith on the wide ocean —not by those who had been watching with divided hearts for a Catholic revolution.

March went by, and sure intelligence came that the Armada was not dissolving. Again Drake prayed the Queen to let him take the *Revenge* and the Western adventurers down to Lisbon; but the commissioners wrote full of hope from Ostend, and Elizabeth was afraid 'the King of Spain might take it ill.' She found fault with

Drake's expenses. She charged him with wasting her ammunition in target practice. She had it doled out to him in driblets, and allowed no more than would serve for a day and a half's service. She kept a sharp hand on the victualling houses. April went, and her four finest ships—the *Triumph*, the *Victory*, the *Elizabeth Jonas*, and the *Bear*—were still with sails unbent, 'keeping Chatham church.' She said they would not be wanted and it would be waste of money to refit them. Again she was forced to yield at last, and the four ships were got to sea in time, the workmen in the yards making up for the delay; but she had few enough when her whole fleet was out upon the Channel, and but for the privateers there would have been an ill reckoning when the trial came. The Armada was coming now. There was no longer a doubt of it. Lord Henry Seymour was left with five Queen's ships and thirty London adventurers to watch Parma and the Narrow Seas. Howard, carrying his own flag in the *Ark Raleigh*, joined Drake at Plymouth with seventeen others.

Still the numbing hand of his mistress pursued

him. Food supplies had been issued to the
middle of June, and no more was to be allowed.
The weather was desperate—wildest summer ever
known. The south-west gales brought the
Atlantic rollers into the Sound. Drake lay
inside, perhaps behind the island which bears his
name. Howard rode out the gales under Mount
Edgecumbe, the days going by and the provisions
wasting. The rations were cut down to make
the stores last longer. Owing to the many
changes the crews had been hastily raised. They
were ill-clothed, ill-provided every way, but they
complained of nothing, caught fish to mend their
mess dinners, and prayed only for the speedy
coming of the enemy. Even Howard's heart
failed him now. English sailors would do what
could be done by man, but they could not fight
with famine. 'Awake, Madam,' he wrote to the
Queen, 'awake, for the love of Christ, and see the
villainous treasons round about you.' He goaded
her into ordering supplies for one more month,
but this was to be positively the last. The
victuallers inquired if they should make further
preparations. She answered peremptorily, 'No'·

and again the weeks ran on. The contractors, it seemed, had caught her spirit, for the beer which had been furnished for the fleet turned sour, and those who drank it sickened. The officers, on their own responsibility, ordered wine and arrow-root for the sick out of Plymouth, to be called to a sharp account when all was over. Again the rations were reduced. Four weeks' allowance was stretched to serve for six, and still the Spaniards did not come. So England's forlorn hope was treated at the crisis of her destiny. The preparations on land were scarcely better. The militia had been called out. A hundred thousand men had given their names, and the stations had been arranged where they were to assemble if the enemy attempted a landing. But there were no reserves, no magazines of arms, no stores or tents, no requisites for an army save the men themselves and what local resources could furnish. For a general the Queen had chosen the Earl of Leicester, who might have the merit of fidelity to herself, but otherwise was the worst fitted that she could have found in her whole dominions; and the Prince of Parma was coming, if he came at all, at the head of the best-provided and best-disciplined troops in Europe. The hope of England at that moment was in her patient suffering sailors at Plymouth. Each morning they looked out passionately for the Spanish sails. Time was a worse enemy than the galleons. The six weeks would be soon gone, and the Queen's ships must then leave the seas if the crews were not to starve. Drake had certain news that the Armada had sailed. Where was it? Once he dashed out as far as Ushant, but turned back, lest it should pass him in the night and find Plymouth undefended; and smaller grew the messes and leaner and paler the seamen's faces. Still not a man murmured or gave in. They had no leisure to be sick.

The last week of July had now come. There were half-rations for one week more, and powder for two days' fighting. That was all. On so light a thread such mighty issues were now depending. On Friday, the 23rd, the Armada had started for the second time, the numbers undiminished; religious fervour burning again, and heart and hope high as ever. Saturday, Sunday, and

Monday they sailed on with a smooth sea and soft south winds, and on Monday night the Duke found himself at the Channel mouth with all his flock about him. Tuesday morning the wind shifted to the north, then backed to the west, and blew hard. The sea got up, broke into the stern galleries of the galleons, and sent the galleys looking for shelter in French harbours. The fleet hove to for a couple of days, till the weather mended. On Friday afternoon they sighted the Lizard and formed into fighting order; the Duke in the centre, Alonzo de Leyva leading in a vessel of his own called the *Rata Coronada*, Don Martin de Recalde covering the rear. The entire line stretched to about seven miles.

The sacred banner was run up to the masthead of the *San Martin*. Each ship saluted with all her guns, and every man—officer, noble, seaman, or slave—knelt on the decks at a given signal to commend themselves to Mary and her Son. We shall miss the meaning of this high epic story if we do not realise that both sides had the most profound conviction that they were fighting the battle of the Almighty. Two principles, freedom and authority, were contending for the guidance of mankind. In the evening the Duke sent off two fast fly-boats to Parma to announce his arrival in the Channel, with another reporting progress to Philip, and saying that till he heard from the Prince he meant to stop at the Isle of Wight. It is commonly said that his officers advised him to go in and take Plymouth. There is no evidence for this. The island would have been a far more useful position for them.

At dark that Friday night the beacons were seen blazing all up the coast and inland on the tops of the hills. They crept on slowly through Saturday, with reduced canvas, feeling their way —not a sail to be seen. At midnight a pinnace brought in a fishing-boat, from which they learnt that on the sight of the signal fires the English had come out that morning from Plymouth. Presently, when the moon rose, they saw sails passing between them and the land. With day-break the whole scene became visible, and the curtain lifted on the first act of the drama. The Armada was between Rame Head and the Eddy-stone, or a little to the west of it. Plymouth Sound

was right open to their left. The breeze, which
had dropped in the night, was freshening from the
south-west, and right ahead of them, outside the
Mew Stone, were eleven ships manœuvring to
recover the wind. Towards the land were some
forty others, of various sizes, and this formed, as
far as they could see, the whole English force. In
numbers the Spaniards were nearly three to one.
In the size of the ships there was no comparison.
With these advantages the Duke decided to
engage, and a signal was made to hold the wind
and keep the enemy apart. The eleven ships
ahead were Howard's squadron ; those inside were
Drake and the adventurers. With some surprise
the Spanish officers saw Howard reach easily to
windward out of range and join Drake. The
whole English fleet then passed out close-hauled
in line behind them and swept along their rear,
using guns more powerful than theirs and pouring
in broadsides from safe distance with deadly effect.
Recalde, with Alonzo de Leyva and Oquendo, who
came to his help, tried desperately to close; but
they could make nothing of it. They were out-
sailed and out-cannoned. The English fired five

shots to one of theirs, and the effect was the more
destructive because, as with Rodney's action at
Dominica, the galleons were crowded with troops,
and shot and splinters told terribly among them.

The experience was new and not agreeable.
Recalde's division was badly cut up, and a Spaniard
present observes that certain officers showed cowardice—a hit at the Duke, who had kept out of
fire.   The action lasted till four in the afternoon.
The wind was then freshening fast and the sea
rising.   Both fleets had by this time passed the
Sound, and the Duke, seeing that nothing could
be done, signalled to bear away up Channel, the
English following two miles astern.   Recalde's
own ship had been an especial sufferer.   She was
observed to be leaking badly, to drop behind, and
to be in danger of capture.   Pedro de Valdez wore
round to help him in the *Capitana*, of the Andalusian squadron, fouled the *Santa Catalina* in
turning, broke his bowsprit and foretopmast, and
became unmanageable.   The Andalusian *Capitana* was one of the finest ships in the Spanish
fleet, and Don Pedro one of the ablest and most
popular commanders.   She had 500 men on

board, a large sum of money, and, among other treasures, a box of jewel-hilted swords, which Philip was sending over to the English Catholic peers. But it was growing dark. Sea and sky looked ugly. The Duke was flurried, and signalled to go on and leave Don Pedro to his fate. Alonzo de Leyva and Oquendo rushed on board the *San Martin* to protest. It was no use. Diego Florez said he could not risk the safety of the fleet for a single officer. The deserted *Capitana* made a brave defence, but could not save herself, and fell, with the jewelled swords, 50,000 ducats, and a welcome supply of powder, into Drake's hands.

Off the Start there was a fresh disaster. Everyone was in ill-humour. A quarrel broke out between the soldiers and seamen in Oquendo's galleon. He was himself still absent. Some wretch or other flung a torch into the powder magazine and jumped overboard. The deck was blown off, and 200 men along with it.

Two such accidents following an unsuccessful engagement did not tend to reconcile the Spaniards to the Duke's command. Pedro de

Valdez was universally loved and honoured, and his desertion in the face of an enemy so inferior in numbers was regarded as scandalous poltroonery. Monday morning broke heavily. The wind was gone, but there was still a considerable swell. The English were hull down behind. The day was spent in repairing damages and nailing lead over the shot-holes. Recalde was moved to the front, to be out of harm's way, and De Leyva took his post in the rear.

At sunset they were outside Portland. The English had come up within a league; but it was now dead calm, and they drifted apart in the tide. The Duke thought of nothing, but at midnight the Spanish officers stirred him out of his sleep to urge him to set his great galleasses to work; now was their chance. The dawn brought a chance still better, for it brought an east wind, and the Spaniards had now the weather-gage. Could they once close and grapple with the English ships, their superior numbers would then assure them a victory, and Howard, being to leeward and inshore, would have to pass through the middle of the Spanish line to recover his advantage. However,

it was the same story. The Spaniards could not
use an opportunity when they had one. New-
modelled for superiority of sailing, the English
ships had the same advantage over the galleons as
the steam cruisers would have over the old three-
deckers. While the breeze held they went where
they pleased. The Spaniards were out-sailed, out-
matched, crushed by guns of longer range than
theirs. Their own shot flew high over the low
English hulls, while every ball found its way
through their own towering sides. This time the
San Martin was in the thick of it. Her double
timbers were ripped and torn; the holy standard
was cut in two; the water poured through the
shot-holes. The men lost their nerve. In such
ships as had no gentlemen on board notable signs
were observed of flinching.

At the end of that day's fighting the English
powder gave out. Two days' service had been the
limit of the Queen's allowance. Howard had
pressed for a more liberal supply at the last
moment, and had received the characteristic
answer that he must state precisely how much he
wanted before more could be sent. The lighting

of the beacons had quickened the official pulse a
little. A small addition had been despatched to
Weymouth or Poole, and no more could be done
till it arrived. The Duke, meanwhile, was left to
smooth his ruffled plumes and drift on upon his
way. But by this time England was awake.
Fresh privateers, with powder, meat, bread, fruit,
anything that they could bring, were pouring out
from the Dorsetshire harbours. Sir George Carey
had come from the Needles in time to share the
honours of the last battle, 'round shot,' as he said,
'flying thick as musket balls in a skirmish on
land.'

The Duke had observed uneasily from the
San Martin's deck that his pursuers were growing
numerous. He had made up his mind definitely
to go for the Isle of Wight, shelter his fleet in the
Solent, land 10,000 men in the island, and stand
on his defence till he heard from Parma. He
must fight another battle; but, cut up as he had
been, he had as yet lost but two ships, and those
by accident. He might fairly hope to force his
way in with help from above, for which he had
special reason to look in the next engagement.

Wednesday was a breathless calm. The English were taking in their supplies. The Armada lay still, repairing damages. Thursday would be St. Dominic's Day. St. Dominic belonged to the Duke's own family, and was his patron saint. St. Dominic he felt sure, would now stand by his kinsman.

The morning broke with a light air. The English would be less able to move, and with the help of the galleasses he might hope to come to close quarters at last. Howard seemed inclined to give him his wish. With just wind enough to move the Lord Admiral led in the *Ark Raleigh* straight down on the Spanish centre. The *Ark* outsailed her consorts and found herself alone with the galleons all round her. At that moment the wind dropped. The Spanish boarding-parties were at their posts. The tops were manned with musketeers, the grappling irons all prepared to fling into the *Ark's* rigging. In imagination the English admiral was their own. But each day's experience was to teach them a new lesson. Eleven boats dropped from the *Ark's* sides and took her in tow. The breeze rose again

as she began to move. Her sails filled, and
she slipped away through the water, leaving
the Spaniards as if they were at anchor, staring
in helpless amazement. The wind brought up
Drake and the rest, and then began again the
terrible cannonade from which the Armada had
already suffered so frightfully. It seemed that
morning as if the English were using guns of
even heavier metal than on either of the preceding
days. The armament had not been changed.
The growth was in their own frightened imagination. The Duke had other causes for uneasiness.
His own magazines were also giving out under
the unexpected demands upon them. One battle
was the utmost which he had looked for. He
had fought three, and the end was no nearer than
before. With resolution he might still have
made his way into St. Helen's roads, for the
English were evidently afraid to close with him.
But when St. Dominic, too, failed him he lost his
head. He lost his heart, and losing heart he
lost all. In the Solent he would have been comparatively safe, and he could easily have taken
the Isle of Wight; but his one thought now was

to find safety under Parma's gaberdine and make
for Calais or Dunkirk. He supposed Parma to
have already embarked, on hearing of his coming,
with a second armed fleet, and in condition for
immediate action. He sent on another pinnace,
pressing for help, pressing for ammunition, and
fly-boats to protect the galleons; and Parma was
himself looking to be supplied from the Armada,
with no second fleet at all, only a flotilla of river
barges which would need a week's work to be
prepared for the crossing.

　　Philip had provided a splendid fleet, a splendid
army, and the finest sailors in the world except
the English. He had failed to realise that the
grandest preparations are useless with a fool to
command. The poor Duke was less to blame
than his master. An office had been thrust upon
him for which he knew that he had not a single
qualification. His one anxiety was to find Parma,
lay the weight on Parma's shoulders, and so have
done with it.

　　On Friday he was left alone to make his way
up Channel towards the French shore. The
English still followed, but he counted that in

Calais roads he would be in French waters, where they would not dare to meddle with him. They would then, he thought, go home and annoy him no further. As he dropped anchor in the dusk outside Calais on Saturday evening he saw, to his disgust, that the *endemoniada gente*—the infernal devils—as he called them, had brought up at the same moment with himself, half a league astern of him. His one trust was in the Prince of Parma, and Parma at any rate was now within touch.

LECTURE IX

DEFEAT OF THE ARMADA

IN the gallery at Madrid there is a picture, painted by Titian, representing the Genius of Spain coming to the delivery of the afflicted Bride of Christ. Titian was dead, but the temper of the age survived, and in the study of that great picture you will see the spirit in which the Spanish nation had set out for the conquest of England. The scene is the seashore. The Church a naked Andromeda, with dishevelled hair, fastened to the trunk of an ancient disbranched tree. The cross lies at her feet, the cup overturned, the serpents of heresy biting at her from behind with uplifted crests. Coming on before a leading breeze is the sea monster, the Moslem fleet, eager for their prey; while in front is Perseus, the Genius of Spain, banner in hand, with the legions of the faithful laying not raiment before him, but shield and helmet, the apparel of war for the Lady of Nations to clothe herself with strength and smite her foes.

In the Armada the crusading enthusiasm had reached its point and focus. England was the stake to which the Virgin, the daughter of Sion, was bound in captivity. Perseus had come at last in the person of the Duke of Medina Sidonia, and with him all that was best and brightest in the countrymen of Cervantes, to break her bonds and replace her on her throne. They had sailed into the Channel in pious hope, with the blessed banner waving over their heads.

To be the executor of the decrees of Providence is a lofty ambition, but men in a state of high emotion overlook the precautions which are not to be dispensed with even on the sublimest of errands. Don Quixote, when he set out to redress the wrongs of humanity, forgot that a change of linen might be necessary, and that he must take money with him to pay his hotel bills. Philip II., in sending the Armada to England, and confident in supernatural protection, imagined an unresisted

T

triumphal procession. He forgot that contractors might be rascals, that water four months in the casks in a hot climate turned putrid, and that putrid water would poison his ships' companies, though his crews were companies of angels. He forgot that the servants of the evil one might fight for their mistress after all, and that he must send adequate supplies of powder, and, worst forgetfulness of all, that a great naval expedition required a leader who understood his business. Perseus, in the shape of the Duke of Medina Sidonia, after a week of disastrous battles, found himself at the end of it in an exposed roadstead, where he ought never to have been, nine-tenths of his provisions thrown overboard as unfit for food, his ammunition exhausted by the unforeseen demands upon it, the seamen and soldiers harassed and dispirited, officers the whole week without sleep, and the enemy, who had hunted him from Plymouth to Calais, anchored within half a league of him.

Still, after all his misadventures, he had brought the fleet, if not to the North Foreland, yet within a few miles of it, and to outward appearance not materially injured. Two of the galleons had been

taken; a third, the *Santa Aña*, had strayed; and
his galleys had left him, being found too weak for
the Channel sea; but the great armament had
reached its destination substantially uninjured so
far as English eyes could see. Hundreds of men
had been killed and hundreds more wounded, and
the spirit of the rest had been shaken. But the
loss of life could only be conjectured on board the
English fleet. The English admiral could only
see that the Duke was now in touch with Parma.
Parma, they knew, had an army at Dunkirk with
him, which was to cross to England. He had
been collecting men, barges, and transports all the
winter and spring, and the backward state of
Parma's preparations could not be anticipated,
still less relied upon. The Calais anchorage was
unsafe; but at that season of the year, especially
after a wet summer, the weather usually settled;
and to attack the Spaniards in a French port might
be dangerous for many reasons. It was uncertain
after the day of the Barricades whether the Duke
of Guise or Henry of Valois was master of France,
and a violation of the neutrality laws might easily
at that moment bring Guise and France into the

field on the Spaniards' side. It was, no doubt,
with some such expectation that the Duke and
his advisers had chosen Calais as the point at
which to bring up. It was now Saturday, the 7th
of August. The Governor of the town came off in
the evening to the *San Martin.* He expressed
surprise to see the Spanish fleet in so exposed a
position, but he was profuse in his offers of service.
Anything which the Duke required should be provided, especially every facility for communicating
with Dunkirk and Parma. The Duke thanked
him, said that he supposed Parma to be already
embarked with his troops, ready for the passage,
and that his own stay in the roads would be but
brief. On Monday morning at latest he expected
that the attempt to cross would be made. The
Governor took his leave, and the Duke, relieved
from his anxieties, was left to a peaceful night.
He was disturbed on the Sunday morning by an
express from Parma informing him that, so far
from being embarked, the army could not be
ready for a fortnight. The barges were not in
condition for sea. The troops were in camp. The
arms and stores were on the quays at Dunkirk.

As for the fly-boats and ammunition which the Duke had asked for, he had none to spare. He had himself looked to be supplied from the Armada. He promised to use his best expedition, but the Duke, meanwhile, must see to the safety of the fleet.

Unwelcome news to a harassed landsman thrust into the position of an admiral and eager to be rid of his responsibilities. If by evil fortune the north-wester should come down upon him, with the shoals and sandbanks close under his lee, he would be in a bad way. Nor was the view behind him calculated for comfort. There lay the enemy almost within gunshot, who, though scarcely more than half his numbers, had hunted him like a pack of bloodhounds, and, worse than all, in double strength; for the Thames squadron — three Queen's ships and thirty London adventurers— under Lord H. Seymour and Sir John Hawkins, had crossed in the night. There they were between him and Cape Grisnez, and the reinforcement meant plainly enough that mischief was in the wind.

After a week so trying the Spanish crews

would have been glad of a Sunday's rest if they could have had it; but the rough handling which they had gone through had thrown everything into disorder. The sick and wounded had to be cared for, torn rigging looked to, splintered timbers mended, decks scoured, and guns and arms cleaned up and put to rights. And so it was that no rest could be allowed; so much had to be done, and so busy was everyone, that the usual rations were not served out and the Sunday was kept as a fast. In the afternoon the stewards went ashore for fresh meat and vegetables. They came back with their boats loaded, and the prospect seemed a little less gloomy. Suddenly, as the Duke and a group of officers were watching the English fleet from the *San Martin's* poop deck, a small smart pinnace, carrying a gun in her bow, shot out from Howard's lines, bore down on the *San Martin*, sailed round her, sending in a shot or two as she passed, and went off unhurt. The Spanish officers could not help admiring such airy impertinence. Hugo de Monçada sent a ball after the pinnace, which went through her mainsail, but did no damage, and the

pinnace again disappeared behind the English
ships.

So a Spanish officer describes the scene. The
English story says nothing of the pinnace; but
she doubtless came and went as the Spaniard
says, and for sufficient purpose. The English,
too, were in straits, though the Duke did not
dream of it. You will remember that the last
supplies which the Queen had allowed to the fleet
had been issued in the middle of June. They
were to serve for a month, and the contractors
were forbidden to prepare more. The Queen had
clung to her hope that her differences with Philip
were to be settled by the Commission at Ostend;
and she feared that if Drake and Howard were
too well furnished they would venture some fresh
rash stroke on the coast of Spain, which might
mar the negotiations. Their month's provisions
had been stretched to serve for six weeks, and
when the Armada appeared but two full days'
rations remained. On these they had fought
their way up Channel. Something had been
brought out by private exertion on the Dorsetshire coast, and Seymour had, perhaps, brought a

little more. But they were still in extremity.
The contractors had warned the Government that
they could provide nothing without notice, and
notice had not been given. The adventurers
were in better state, having been equipped by
private owners. But the Queen's ships in a day
or two more must either go home or their crews
would be starving. They had been on reduced
rations for near two months. Worse than that,
they were still poisoned by the sour beer. The
Queen had changed her mind so often, now
ordering the fleet to prepare for sea, then re-
calling her instructions and paying off the men,
that those whom Howard had with him had been
enlisted in haste, had come on board as they were,
and their clothes were hanging in rags on them.
The fighting and the sight of the flying Spaniards
were meat and drink, and clothing too, and had
made them careless of all else. There was no
fear of mutiny; but there was a limit to the
toughest endurance. If the Armada was left
undisturbed a long struggle might be still before
them. The enemy would recover from its flurry,
and Parma would come out from Dunkirk. To

attack them directly in French waters might lead
to perilous complications, while delay meant
famine. The Spanish fleet had to be started
from the roads in some way. Done it must be,
and done immediately.

Then, on that same Sunday afternoon a
memorable council of war was held in the *Ark's*
main cabin. Howard, Drake, Seymour, Hawkins,
Martin Frobisher, and two or three others met to
consult, knowing that on them at that moment
the liberties of England were depending. Their
resolution was taken promptly. There was no
time for talk. After nightfall a strong flood tide
would be setting up along shore to the Spanish
anchorage. They would try what could be done
with fire-ships, and the excursion of the pinnace,
which was taken for bravado, was probably for a
survey of the Armada's exact position. Meantime eight useless vessels were coated with pitch
—hulls, spars, and rigging. Pitch was poured on
the decks and over the sides, and parties were
told off to steer them to their destination and
then fire and leave them.

The hours stole on, and twilight passed into

dark. The night was without a moon. The
Duke paced his deck late with uneasy sense of
danger. He observed lights moving up and
down the English lines, and imagining that the
endemoniada gente—the infernal devils—might be
up to mischief, ordered a sharp look-out. A faint
westerly air was curling the water, and towards
midnight the watchers on board the galleons
made out dimly several ships which seemed to
be drifting down upon them. Their experience
since the action off Plymouth had been so strange
and unlooked for that anything unintelligible
which the English did was alarming.

The phantom forms drew nearer, and were
almost among them when they broke into a blaze
from water-line to truck, and the two fleets were
seen by the lurid light of the conflagration ; the
anchorage, the walls and windows of Calais, and
the sea shining red far as eye could reach, as
if the ocean itself was burning. Among the
dangers which they might have to encounter,
English fireworks had been especially dreaded
by the Spaniards. Fire-ships—a fit device of
heretics—had worked havoc among the Spanish

troops, when the bridge was blown up, at
Antwerp. They imagined that similar infernal
machines were approaching the Armada. A
capable commander would have sent a few
launches to grapple the burning hulks, which
of course were now deserted, and tow them
out of harm's way. Spanish sailors were not
cowards, and would not have flinched from duty
because it might be dangerous; but the Duke
and Diego Florez lost their heads again. A
signal gun from the *San Martin* ordered the
whole fleet to slip their cables and stand out
to sea.

Orders given in panic are doubly unwise, for
they spread the terror in which they originate.
The danger from the fire-ships was chiefly from
the effect on the imagination, for they appear to
have drifted by and done no real injury. And it
speaks well for the seamanship and courage of
the Spaniards that they were able, crowded
together as they were, at midnight and in sudden
alarm to set their canvas and clear out without
running into one another. They buoyed their
cables, expecting to return for them at daylight,

and with only a single accident, to be mentioned directly, they executed successfully a really difficult manœuvre.

The Duke was delighted with himself. The fire-ships burnt harmlessly out. He had baffled the inventions of the *endemoniada gente*. He brought up a league outside the harbour, and supposed that the whole Armada had done the same. Unluckily for himself, he found it at day-light divided into two bodies. The *San Martin* with forty of the best appointed of the galleons were riding together at their anchors. The rest, two-thirds of the whole, having no second anchors ready, and inexperienced in Channel tides and currents, had been lying to. The west wind was blowing up. Without seeing where they were going they had drifted to leeward, and were two leagues off, towards Gravelines, dangerously near the shore. The Duke was too ignorant to realise the full peril of his situation. He signalled to them to return and rejoin him. As the wind and tide stood it was impossible. He proposed to follow them. The pilots told him that if he did the whole fleet might be lost on the banks.

Towards the land the look of things was not more encouraging.

One accident only had happened the night before. The *Capitana* galleass, with Don Hugo de Monçada and eight hundred men on board, had fouled her helm in a cable in getting under way and had become unmanageable. The galley slaves disobeyed orders, or else Don Hugo was as incompetent as his commander-in-chief. The galleass had gone on the sands, and as the tide ebbed had fallen over on her side. Howard, seeing her condition, had followed her in the *Ark* with four or five other of the Queen's ships, and was furiously attacking her with his boats, careless of neutrality laws. Howard's theory was, as he said, to pluck the feathers one by one from the Spaniard's wing, and here was a feather worth picking up. The galleass was the most splendid vessel of her kind afloat, Don Hugo one of the greatest of Spanish grandees.

Howard was making a double mistake. He took the galleass at last, after three hours' fighting. Don Hugo was killed by a musket ball. The vessel was plundered, and Howard's

men took possession, meaning to carry her away
when the tide rose. The French authorities
ordered him off, threatening to fire upon him;
and after wasting the forenoon, he was obliged
at last to leave her where she lay. Worse than
this, he had lost three precious hours, and had
lost along with them, in the opinion of the
Prince of Parma, the honours of the great day.

Drake and Hawkins knew better than to
waste time plucking single feathers. The fire-
ships had been more effective than they could
have dared to hope. The enemy was broken up.
The Duke was shorn of half his strength, and
the Lord had delivered him into their hand. He
had got under way, still signalling wildly, and
uncertain in which direction to turn. His un-
certainties were ended for him by seeing Drake
bearing down upon him with the whole English
fleet, save those which were loitering about the
galleass. The English had now the advantage of
numbers. The superiority of their guns he knew
already, and their greater speed allowed him no
hope to escape a battle. Forty ships alone were
left to him to defend the banner of the crusade

and the honour of Castile; but those forty were
the largest and the most powerfully armed and
manned that he had, and on board them were
Oquendo, De Leyva, Recalde, and Bretandona,
the best officers in the Spanish navy next to the
lost Don Pedro.

It was now or never for England. The scene
of the action which was to decide the future of
Europe was between Calais and Dunkirk, a few
miles off shore, and within sight of Parma's
camp. There was no more manœuvring for the
weather-gage, no more fighting at long range.
Drake dashed straight upon his prey as the falcon
stoops upon its quarry. A chance had fallen to
him which might never return; not for the vain
distinction of carrying prizes into English ports,
not for the ray of honour which would fall on him
if he could carry off the sacred banner itself and
hang it in the Abbey at Westminster, but a
chance so to handle the Armada that it should
never be seen again in English waters, and deal
such a blow on Philip that the Spanish Empire
should reel with it. The English ships had the
same superiority over the galleons which steamers

have now over sailing vessels. They had twice
the speed; they could lie two points nearer to
the wind. Sweeping round them at cable's
length, crowding them in one upon the other, yet
never once giving them a chance to grapple, they
hurled in their cataracts of round shot. Short as
was the powder supply, there was no sparing it
that morning. The hours went on, and still the
battle raged, if battle it could be called where
the blows were all dealt on one side and the
suffering was all on the other. Never on sea or
land did the Spaniards show themselves worthier
of their great name than on that day. But from
the first they could do nothing. It was said
afterwards in Spain that the Duke showed the
white feather, that he charged his pilot to keep
him out of harm's way, that he shut himself up
in his cabin, buried in woolpacks, and so on.
The Duke had faults enough, but poltroonery was
not one of them. He, who till he entered the
English Channel had never been in action on sea
or land, found himself, as he said, in the midst
of the most furious engagement recorded in the
history of the world. As to being out of harm's

way, the standard at his masthead drew the
hottest of the fire upon him. The *San Martin's*
timbers were of oak and a foot thick, but the
shot, he said, went through them enough to
shatter a rock. Her deck was a slaughterhouse;
half his company were killed or wounded, and
no more would have been heard or seen of the
San Martin or her commander had not Oquendo
and De Leyva pushed in to the rescue and
enabled him to creep away under their cover.
He himself saw nothing more of the action after
this. The smoke, he said, was so thick that he
could make out nothing, even from his masthead.
But all round it was but a repetition of the same
scene. The Spanish shot flew high, as before,
above the low English hulls, and they were
themselves helpless butts to the English guns.
And it is noticeable and supremely creditable to
them that not a single galleon struck her colours.
One of them, after a long duel with an Englishman, was on the point of sinking. An English
officer, admiring the courage which the Spaniards
had shown, ran out upon his bowsprit, told them
that they had done all which became men, and

U

urged them to surrender and save their lives.
For answer they cursed the English as cowards
and chickens because they refused to close. The
officer was shot. His fall brought a last broadside
on them, which finished the work. They went
down, and the water closed over them. Rather
death to the soldiers of the Cross than surrender
to a heretic.

The deadly hail rained on. In some ships
blood was seen streaming out of the scupper-
holes. Yet there was no yielding; all ranks
showed equal heroism. The priests went up and
down in the midst of the carnage, holding the
crucifix before the eyes of the dying. At midday
Howard came up to claim a second share in a
victory which was no longer doubtful. Towards
the afternoon the Spanish fire slackened. Their
powder was gone, and they could make no return
to the cannonade which was still overwhelming
them. They admitted freely afterwards that if
the attack had been continued but two hours
more they must all have struck or gone ashore.
But the English magazines were empty also; the
last cartridge was shot away, and the battle

ended from mere inability to keep it up. It had been fought on both sides with peculiar determination. In the English there was the accumulated resentment of thirty years of menace to their country and their creed, with the enemy in tangible shape at last to be caught and grappled with; in the Spanish, the sense that if their cause had not brought them the help they looked for from above, the honour and faith of Castile should not suffer in their hands.

It was over. The English drew off, regretting that their thrifty mistress had limited their means of fighting for her, and so obliged them to leave their work half done. When the cannon ceased the wind rose, the smoke rolled away, and in the level light of the sunset they could see the results of the action.

A galleon in Recalde's squadron was sinking with all hands. The *San Philip* and the *San Matteo* were drifting dismasted towards the Dutch coast, where they were afterwards wrecked. Those which were left with canvas still showing were crawling slowly after their comrades who had not been engaged, the spars and rigging so cut up that they could scarce bear their sails. The loss of life could only be conjectured, but it had been obviously terrible. The nor'-wester was blowing up and was pressing the wounded ships upon the shoals, from which, if it held, it seemed impossible in their crippled state they would be able to work off.

In this condition Drake left them for the night, not to rest, but from any quarter to collect, if he could, more food and powder. The snake had been scotched, but not killed. More than half the great fleet were far away, untouched by shot, perhaps able to fight a second battle if they recovered heart. To follow, to drive them on the banks if the wind held, or into the North Sea, anywhere so that he left them no chance of joining hands with Parma again, and to use the time before they had rallied from his blows, that was the present necessity. His own poor fellows were famished and in rags; but neither he nor they had leisure to think of themselves. There was but one thought in the whole of them, to be again in chase of the flying foe. Howard was resolute as Drake. All that was possible was swiftly done.

Seymour and the Thames squadron were to stay in the Straits and watch Parma. From every attainable source food and powder were collected for the rest—far short in both ways of what ought to have been, but, as Drake said, ' we were resolved to put on a brag and go on as if we needed nothing.' Before dawn the admiral and he were again off on the chase.

The brag was unneeded. What man could do had been done, and the rest was left to the elements. Never again could Spanish seamen be brought to face the English guns with Medina Sidonia to lead them. They had a fool at their head. The Invisible Powers in whom they had been taught to trust had deserted them. Their confidence was gone and their spirit broken. Drearily the morning broke on the Duke and his consorts the day after the battle. The Armada had collected in the night. The nor'-wester had freshened to a gale, and they were labouring heavily along, making fatal leeway towards the shoals.

It was St. Lawrence's Day, Philip's patron saint, whose shoulder-bone he had lately added to

the treasures of the Escurial; but St. Lawrence
was as heedless as St. Dominic. The *San Martin*
had but six fathoms under her. Those nearer to
the land signalled five, and right before them
they could see the brown foam of the breakers
curling over the sands, while on their weather-
beam, a mile distant and clinging to them like
the shadow of death, were the English ships
which had pursued them from Plymouth like
the dogs of the Furies. The Spanish sailors and
soldiers had been without food since the evening
when they anchored at Calais. All Sunday they
had been at work, no rest allowed them to eat.
On the Sunday night they had been stirred out
of their sleep by the fire-ships. Monday they
had been fighting, and Monday night committing
their dead to the sea. Now they seemed advanc-
ing directly upon inevitable destruction. As the
wind stood there was still room for them to wear
and thus escape the banks, but they would then
have to face the enemy, who seemed only refrain-
ing from attacking them because while they
continued on their present course the winds and
waves would finish the work without help from

man. Recalde, De Leyva, Oquendo, and other officers were sent for to the *San Martin* to consult. Oquendo came last. 'Ah, Señor Oquendo,' said the Duke as the heroic Biscayan stepped on board, 'que haremos?' (what shall we do?) 'Let your Excellency bid load the guns again,' was Oquendo's gallant answer. It could not be. De Leyva himself said that the men would not fight the English again. Florez advised surrender. The Duke wavered. It was said that a boat was actually lowered to go off to Howard and make terms, and that Oquendo swore that if the boat left the *San Martin* on such an errand he would fling Florez into the sea. Oquendo's advice would have, perhaps, been the safest if the Duke could have taken it. There were still seventy ships in the Armada little hurt. The English were 'bragging,' as Drake said, and in no condition themselves for another serious engagement. But the temper of the entire fleet made a courageous course impossible. There was but one Oquendo. Discipline was gone. The soldiers in their desperation had taken the command out of the hands of the seamen. Officers and men alike abandoned hope, and, with no human prospect of salvation left to them, they flung themselves on their knees upon the decks and prayed the Almighty to have pity on them. But two weeks were gone since they had knelt on those same decks on the first sight of the English shore to thank Him for having brought them so far on an enterprise so glorious. Two weeks; and what weeks! Wrecked, torn by cannon shot, ten thousand of them dead or dying—for this was the estimated loss by battle —the survivors could now but pray to be delivered from a miserable death by the elements. In cyclones the wind often changes suddenly back from north-west to west, from west to south. At that moment, as if in answer to their petition, one of these sudden shifts of wind saved them from the immediate peril. The gale backed round to S.S.W., and ceased to press them on the shoals. They could ease their sheets, draw off into open water, and steer a course up the middle of the North Sea.

So only that they went north, Drake was content to leave them unmolested. Once away into the high latitudes they might go where they

would. Neither Howard nor he, in the low state
of their own magazines, desired any unnecessary
fighting. If the Armada turned back they must
close with it. If it held its present course they
must follow it till they could be assured it would
communicate no more for that summer with the
Prince of Parma. Drake thought they would
perhaps make for the Baltic or some port in
Norway. They would meet no hospitable reception from either Swedes or Danes, but they would
probably try. One only imminent danger remained to be provided against. If they turned
into the Forth, it was still possible for the
Spaniards to redeem their defeat, and even yet
shake Elizabeth's throne. Among the many
plans which had been formed for the invasion
of England, a landing in Scotland had long
been the favourite. Guise had always preferred
Scotland when it was intended that Guise should
be the leader. Santa Cruz had been in close
correspondence with Guise on this very subject,
and many officers in the Armada must have
been acquainted with Santa Cruz's views. The
Scotch Catholic nobles were still savage at Mary

Stuart's execution, and had the Armada anchored in Leith Roads with twenty thousand men, half a million ducats, and a Santa Cruz at its head, it might have kindled a blaze at that moment from John o' Groat's Land to the Border.

But no such purpose occurred to the Duke of Medina Sidonia. He probably knew nothing at all of Scotland or its parties. Among the many deficiencies which he had pleaded to Philip as unfitting him for the command, he had said that Santa Cruz had acquaintances among the English and Scotch peers. He had himself none. The small information which he had of anything did not go beyond his orange gardens and his tunny fishing. His chief merit was that he was conscious of his incapacity; and, detesting a service into which he had been fooled by a hysterical nun, his only anxiety was to carry home the still considerable fleet which had been trusted to him without further loss. Beyond Scotland and the Scotch Isles there was the open ocean, and in the open ocean there were no sand-banks and no English guns. Thus, with all sail set he went on before the wind. Drake and

Howard attended him till they had seen him past the Forth, and knew then that there was no more to fear. It was time to see to the wants of their own poor fellows, who had endured so patiently and fought so magnificently. On the 13th of August they saw the last of the Armada, turned back, and made their way to the Thames.

But the story has yet to be told of the final fate of the great 'enterprise of England' (the 'empresa de Inglaterra'), the object of so many prayers, on which the hopes of the Catholic world had been so long and passionately fixed. It had been ostentatiously a religious crusade. The preparations had been attended with peculiar solemnities. In the eyes of the faithful it was to be the execution of Divine justice on a wicked princess and a wicked people. In the eyes of millions whose convictions were less decided it was an appeal to God's judgment to decide between the Reformation and the Pope. There was an appropriateness, therefore, if due to accident, that other causes besides the action of man should have combined in its overthrow.

The Spaniards were experienced sailors; a

voyage round the Orkneys and round Ireland to
Spain might be tedious, but at that season of the
year need not have seemed either dangerous or
difficult. On inquiry, however, it was found that
the condition of the fleet was seriously alarming.
The provisions placed on board at Lisbon had
been found unfit for food, and almost all had
been thrown into the sea. The fresh stores
taken in at Corunna had been consumed, and it
was found that at the present rate there would
be nothing left in a fortnight. Worse than all,
the water-casks refilled there had been carelessly
stowed. They had been shot through in the fighting and were empty; while of clothing or other
comforts for the cold regions which they were
entering no thought had been taken. The mules
and horses were flung overboard, and Scotch
smacks, which had followed the retreating fleet,
reported that they had sailed for miles through
floating carcases.

The rations were reduced for each man to a
daily half-pound of biscuit, a pint of water, and
a pint of wine. Thus, sick and hungry, the
wounded left to the care of a medical officer, who

went from ship to ship, the subjects of so many
prayers were left to encounter the climate of the
North Atlantic. The Duke blamed all but himself; he hanged one poor captain for neglect of
orders, and would have hanged another had he
dared; but his authority was gone. They passed
the Orkneys in a single body. They then parted,
it was said in a fog; but each commander had to
look out for himself and his men. In many ships
water must be had somewhere, or they would die.
The *San Martin*, with sixty consorts, went north
to the sixtieth parallel. From that height the
pilots promised to take them down clear of the
coast. The wind still clung to the west, each
day blowing harder than the last. When they
braced round to it their wounded spars gave
way. Their rigging parted. With the greatest
difficulty they made at last sufficient offing, and
rolled down somehow out of sight of land, dipping
their yards in the enormous seas. Of the rest,
one or two went down among the Western Isles
and became wrecks there, their crews, or part of
them, making their way through Scotland to
Flanders. Others went north to Shetland or the

Faroe Islands. Between thirty and forty were
tempted in upon the Irish coasts. There were
Irishmen in the fleet, who must have told them
that they would find the water there for which
they were perishing, safe harbours, and a friendly
Catholic people; and they found either harbours
which they could not reach or sea-washed sands
and reefs. They were all wrecked at various
places between Donegal and the Blaskets. Something like eight thousand half-drowned wretches
struggled on shore alive. Many were gentlemen,
richly dressed, with velvet coats, gold chains, and
rings. The common sailors and soldiers had been
paid their wages before they started, and each
had a bag of ducats lashed to his waist when he
landed through the surf. The wild Irish of
the coast, tempted by the booty, knocked un-
known numbers of them on the head with their
battle-axes, or stripped them naked and left them
to die of the cold. On one long sand strip in Sligo
an English officer counted eleven hundred bodies,
and he heard that there were as many more a
few miles distant.

The better-educated of the Ulster chiefs, the

O'Rourke and O'Donnell, hurried down to stop
the butchery and spare Ireland the shame of
murdering helpless Catholic friends. Many—how
many cannot be said — found protection in
their castles. But even so it seemed as if some
inexorable fate pursued all who had sailed
in that doomed expedition. Alonzo de Leyva,
with half a hundred young Spanish nobles of high
rank who were under his special charge, made his
way in a galleass into Killibeg. He was himself
disabled in landing. O'Donnell received and
took care of him and his companions. After
remaining in O'Donnell's castle for a month he
recovered. The weather appeared to mend. The
galleass was patched up, and De Leyva ventured
an attempt to make his way in her to Scotland.
He had passed the worst danger, and Scotland
was almost in sight; but fate would have its
victims. The galleass struck a rock off Dunluce
and went to pieces, and Don Alonzo and the
princely youths who had sailed with him were
washed ashore all dead, to find an unmarked
grave in Antrim.

Most pitiful of all was the fate of those who

fell into the hands of the English garrisons in
Galway and Mayo. Galleons had found their
way into Galway Bay—one of them had reached
Galway itself—the crews half dead with famine
and offering a cask of wine for a cask of water.
The Galway townsmen were human, and tried to
feed and care for them. Most were too far gone
to be revived, and died of exhaustion. Some might
have recovered, but recovered they would be a
danger to the State. The English in the West
of Ireland were but a handful in the midst of a
sullen, half-conquered population. The ashes of
the Desmond rebellion were still smoking, and Dr.
Sanders and his Legatine Commission were fresh
in immediate memory. The defeat of the Armada
in the Channel could only have been vaguely
heard of. All that English officers could have
accurately known must have been that an enormous expedition had been sent to England by
Philip to restore the Pope; and Spaniards, they
found, were landing in thousands in the midst of
them with arms and money; distressed for the
moment, but sure, if allowed time to get their
strength again, to set Connaught in a blaze.

They had no fortresses to hold so many prisoners, no means of feeding them, no men to spare to escort them to Dublin. They were responsible to the Queen's Government for the safety of the country. The Spaniards had not come on any errand of mercy to her or hers. The stern order went out to kill them all wherever they might be found, and two thousand or more were shot, hanged, or put to the sword. Dreadful! Yes, but war itself is dreadful and has its own necessities.

The sixty ships which had followed the *San Martin* succeeded at last in getting round Cape Clear, but in a condition scarcely less miserable than that of their companions who had perished in Ireland. Half their companies died—died of untended wounds, hunger, thirst, and famine fever. The survivors were moving skeletons, more shadows and ghosts than living men, with scarce strength left them to draw a rope or handle a tiller. In some ships there was no water for fourteen days. The weather in the lower latitudes lost part of its violence, or not one of them would have seen Spain again. As it was they

x

drifted on outside Scilly and into the Bay of
Biscay, and in the second week in September
they dropped in one by one. Recalde, with
better success than the rest, made Corunna.
The Duke, not knowing where he was, found
himself in sight of Corunna also. The crew of the
San Martin were prostrate, and could not work
her in. They signalled for help, but none came,
and they dropped away to leeward to Bilbao.
Oquendo had fallen off still farther to Santander,
and the rest of the sixty arrived in the following
days at one or other of the Biscay ports. On
board them, of the thirty thousand who had left
those shores but two months before in high hope
and passionate enthusiasm, nine thousand only
came back alive—if alive they could be called.
It is touching to read in a letter from Bilbao of
their joy at warm Spanish sun, the sight of the
grapes on the white walls, and the taste of fresh
home bread and water again. But it came too
late to save them, and those whose bodies might
have rallied died of broken hearts and disappointed dreams. Santa Cruz's old companions
could not survive the ruin of the Spanish navy.

Recalde died two days after he landed at Bilbao.
Santander was Oquendo's home. He had a wife
and children there, but he refused to see them,
turned his face to the wall, and died too. The
common seamen and soldiers were too weak to
help themselves. They had to be left on board
the poisoned ships till hospitals could be prepared
to take them in. The authorities of Church and
State did all that men could do; but the case
was past help, and before September was out all
but a few hundred needed no further care.

Philip, it must be said for him, spared nothing
to relieve the misery. The widows and orphans
were pensioned by the State. The stroke which
had fallen was received with a dignified submission to the inscrutable purposes of Heaven.
Diego Florez escaped with a brief punishment at
Burgos. None else were punished for faults
which lay chiefly in the King's own presumption
in imagining himself the instrument of Providence.

The Duke thought himself more sinned
against than sinning. He did not die, like
Recalde or Oquendo, seeing no occasion for it.
He flung down his command and retired to his

palace at San Lucan; and so far was Philip from resenting the loss of the Armada on its commander, that he continued him in his governorship of Cadiz, where Essex found him seven years later, and where he ran from Essex as he had run from Drake.

The Spaniards made no attempt to conceal the greatness of their defeat. Unwilling to allow that the Upper Powers had been against them, they set it frankly down to the superior fighting powers of the English.

The English themselves, the Prince of Parma said, were modest in their victory. They thought little of their own gallantry. To them the defeat and destruction of the Spanish fleet was a declaration of the Almighty in the cause of their country and the Protestant faith. Both sides had appealed to Heaven, and Heaven had spoken.

It was the turn of the tide. The wave of the reconquest of the Netherlands ebbed from that moment. Parma took no more towns from the Hollanders. The Catholic peers and gentlemen of England, who had held aloof from the Established Church, waiting *ad illud tempus* for a religious revolution, accepted the verdict of Providence. They discovered that in Anglicanism they could keep the faith of their fathers, yet remain in communion with their Protestant fellow-countrymen, use the same liturgy, and pray in the same temples. For the first time since Elizabeth's father broke the bonds of Rome the English became a united nation, joined in loyal enthusiasm for the Queen, and were satisfied that thenceforward no Italian priest should tithe or toll in her dominions.

But all that, and all that went with it, the passing from Spain to England of the sceptre of the seas, must be left to other lectures, or other lecturers who have more years before them than I. My own theme has been the poor Protestant adventurers who fought through that perilous week in the English Channel and saved their country and their country's liberty.

THE END

Richard Clay & Sons, Limited, London & Bungay.